Hardy to Heaney

▶Twentieth Century Poets◀
▶Introductions and Explanations◀

Oliver & Boyd

© Oliver & Boyd 1986
All rights reserved. No part of this publication
may be reproduced, stored in a retrieval system,
or transmitted in any form or by any means,
electronic, mechanical, photocopying, recording, or
otherwise, without the prior written permission of
the copyright owner.

ISBN 0 05 003958 4

Produced by

■Edited by John Blackburn■

Oliver & Boyd

Oliver & Boyd
Robert Stevenson House
1–3 Baxter's Place
Leith Walk
Edinburgh
EH1 3BB

A Division of Longman Group Limited

ISBN 0 05 003558 4

Produced by Longman Group (F.E.) Ltd
Printed in Hong Kong

Contents

Contributors

Jeffrey Aldridge, Lecturer in English, Moray House College of Education, Edinburgh.   (*Betjeman*)

Victor Ashton, Principal Teacher of English, Currie High School, Edinburgh.   (*Yeats*)

Ian Currie, formerly Senior Lecturer in English and Assistant Principal, Moray House, College of Education, Edinburgh.   (*Larkin* and *Hughes*)

Alan MacGillivray, Senior Lecturer in English, Jordanhill College of Education, Glasgow.   (*Mackay Brown*)

Edwin Morgan, Emeritus Professor of English, University of Glasgow.   (*Williams*)

Robbie Robertson, Senior Curriculum Officer, S.C.D.S., Moray House College of Education, Edinburgh.   (*Hardy* and *War Poetry*)

Ronald Stevenson, Pianist, Musicologist and Broadcaster. (*Wilfred Owen's 'Strange Meeting'*)

Derick Thomson, Professor of Celtic, University of Glasgow.   (*Dialogue on own poetry*)

Geddes Thomson, Principal Teacher of English, Allan Glen's School, Glasgow   (*Heaney*)

Lesley Williams, Principal Teacher of English, Jordanhill College School, Glasgow.   (*Frost*)

Douglas Young, Lecturer in English, Aberdeen College of Education.   (*Muir*)

John Blackburn: Formerly lecturer in English, Moray House College of Education, Edinburgh. Currently, Senior Assistant Examiner, C.S.Y.S. English. (*MacCaig, Morgan, The Gaelic Tradition, Derick Thomson, Iain Crichton Smith*, and Editor)

Introduction

An anthology of poetry, intended for use in senior classes
in secondary schools, was published in 1980 under the
title *Gallery*. The anthology, in which poets from Wyatt
to Heaney were represented, proved popular. This volume of commentary and criticism is now offered as a
companion to that part of *Gallery* which contained a selection of twentieth-century poetry. It will serve also as
a companion to other anthologies of modern poetry.

The reader will find here essays by teachers, lecturers
and writers who act as guides to one or more of the poets
exhibited in *Gallery*. Each guide uses a number of carefully chosen poems (some of which are to be found in
Gallery and some of which are included in the text of the
essays) to highlight the main preoccupations of a particular poet and to draw attention to his manner of writing. In some cases it was thought advisable to provide a
substantial amount of background information about the
poet's life and about the places and events associated
with it. In most cases, however, the reader will find that
attention is quickly focused on the texts of the poems.

It is regretted that, for economic reasons, the present
volume consists of essays on only a selection of the poets
represented in *Gallery*. Of the material originally intended
for publication, a large section, in the form of a dialogue
between Edwin Morgan and myself, on the poetry from
Wyatt to the end of the nineteenth century was the first to
be omitted, in the interests of meeting the more pressing
need for essays on modern and contemporary poets. The
decision to lay aside the past was taken with great
reluctance, since part of the purpose of *Gallery* was to set
poetry of this century against a background of some of
the best known poems of past times. Then, among
twentieth-century poets a selection had to be made. In the
event, it was decided that the essays on Lawrence, Eliot,
Auden, MacDiarmid, R S Thomas and Dylan Thomas and
a dialogue on some of Heaney's later poetry should be

kept for a possible second volume, which could include also the dialogue on pre-twentieth-century poetry. The criteria for making these choices were various. Some items were held back because critical and expository work on the poets concerned is quite readily available elsewhere, some because the level of difficulty of the poetry or the essay was rather above the going average, and some to allow for particular interests and trends that came to my notice. None of the decisions was easy to make.

It will be found that the essays still vary somewhat in level of difficulty. This is inevitable: some poets are more difficult than others and we have proceeded on the assumption that a pupil, or student, capable of appreciating, let us say, Yeats's poetry, will be capable of understanding what our contributor writes about it. It is nevertheless to be emphasised that while a particular essay in its *entirety* might mean more to the teacher than to the young reader, there are to be found in all the essays commentaries on individual poems to which students can be directed for private study and preparation. A glossary of literary terms is provided.

My thanks are due to all those who contributed to this book. Their willingness to conform to a pattern was appreciated, as was their tolerance of editorial suggestions. Particular thanks must be recorded to Edwin Morgan for the part he has played in the course of the last eighteen months – as essayist and ready maker of dialogue. Derick Thomson's help with the prologue to his own poetry was also especially valued. The assistance, in this connection, of Aongas MacNeacail is also gratefully acknowledged. To Seamus Heaney and Helen O'Shea there are due both thanks and commiserations for the script of a dialogue between them which, in the event, had to go the way of Wyatt and the rest, in the meantime at least.

John Blackburn
West Linton, 1985

1. Thomas Hardy
by
ROBBIE ROBERTSON

Reading a collection of Hardy's poetry is always delight-ful. There is a feeling of constant experiment and striving, of being close to a rather diffident, but acute mind, a painter's eye coupled with what is usually an unerring ear for the musical potential of language. One is also aware of inner tensions, doubts and hesitations, with many references to details of his own private life, quite often in his relationships with women, which are tantal-isingly vague and require some knowledge of his life if they are to be fully understood.

Hardy's birth into a working class family on 2nd June 1840, gave him a view of society which in his creative life rarely deserted him, but it was also a birth whose circum-stances, as his success grew, he attempted desperately to hide. What Hardy gained from his family background was not only a powerful sense of the past, transmitted, in the country way, through stories and legends, but also the gift of music: Hardy's father was a fine musician, a popular figure at dances, and from a very early age Hardy himself was encouraged to play – at first an accordion, then the fiddle. The tunes and verse patterns of the bal-lads and of the hymns which he sang in church acted as strong influences on his poetry, giving him that rich melodic sense which even the earliest, and least successful, of his poems reveal. Equally important, however, was the experience of growing up in the country. It gave Hardy a life-long love of nature, of the Dorset countryside, which he re-named Wessex, of the animals who lived there and of the human beings who moved among them.

Hardy was a sickly child (at his birth he was thought to be dead) but his gift for words revealed itself early; there is evidence that he was reading from about the age of three. In the absence of state education it was often necessary for the children of poor parents to educate themselves. This Hardy did, supported by his mother whose influence on him, and on his relationships with women, can be traced throughout his whole life. From the age of fourteen he was attracted to girls who were usually older than himself, and he remembered them into old age. 'To Lizbie Browne', a very happy poem with the flavour of a song, describes and gives the history of one of these targets of a childhood crush. But the relationship was, almost certainly, no more than a crush. Hardy was naturally shy, unhappy in company despite his fiddle-playing at country dances where behaviour was, in general, 'unrestrained'. This shyness haunted Hardy for the whole of his life, and gave his restless society-climbing spirit an uncomfortable edge.

These early experiences can be tasted in a wide range of his poetry. From the earliest poems to the end he was engaged with the idea of love, of emotion, of places and moments which capture the inner meanings not only of the occasion but of the people who inhabit it. He, like us, was also affected by the rejuvenating force that poets such as Wordsworth and Shelley had given to the language. His poetry abounds with descriptions of nature, of its changes and of the creatures – including man – which it affects.

One of the earliest poems, perhaps even the earliest, is 'Domicilium'. The first two verses of the poem describe the house (Hardy's first profession was that of architect):

Red roses, lilacs, variegated box
Are there in plenty, and such hardy flowers
As flourish best untrained. Adjoining these
Are herbs. and esculents; and farther still
A field; then cottages with trees, and last
The distant hills and sky.

But in the third the note changes: the wild heath which
has been pushed back is still there:

Behind, the scene is wilder. Heath and furze
Are everything that seems to grow and thrive
Upon the uneven ground. A stunted thorn
Stands here and there, indeed; and from a pit
An oak uprises, springing from a seed
Dropped by some bird a hundred years ago.

This balance between nature and the garden is, of course,
deeply conventional, very ancient, and takes many forms.
Essentially it is about the beautiful order which human
culture can give but which is always threatened by
human appetites or the 'irrational' actions of nature itself.
It was a theme which moved Hardy profoundly. But the
last lines of the verse signal an interesting change: we are
now taken into the past by way of his grandmother's
reminiscence.

Our house stood quite alone, and those tall firs
And beeches were not planted. Snakes and efts
Swarmed in the summer days, and nightly bats
Would fly about our bedrooms. Heathcroppers
Lived on the hills, and were our only friends;
So wild it was when first we settled here.

This fascination with the way things had been never
deserted Hardy: his love for the people, the landscape,
and the complex histories which his ancestry had handed
down, gives all his adult work a power and an intensity
which it is essential to recognise.

One of the many problems in writing about Hardy's verse is that he wrote so much of it. Not including *The Dynasts* (500 pages of epic drama), and other plays written in verse, he wrote nearly 1000 poems. Not all of them can be dated accurately, and often the only guide to the time of their composition is the personal nature of their messages. But, because Hardy wrote in a masked, allusive style, this guidance is frequently uncertain. He was also in the habit of storing poetry – for decades, sometimes – then quite genuinely re-discovering it, polishing it and publishing with often only the vaguest indication of its date of composition.

Making a fast assessment, it would seem that Hardy wrote a large body of poetry in the 1860's, but scarcely any at all in the following two decades, up to the publication of *Jude the Obscure* in 1896. Thereafter, he stopped writing fiction and concentrated almost entirely on poetry, in one form or another. His first collection, *Wessex Poems*, appeared in 1898 when he was almost sixty. Thereafter he continued to write until his death in 1928, and unlike the majority of poets, his talent did not desert him. His last collection, *Winter Words*, was published after his death, and it contains, as well as poetry written perhaps sixty years earlier, some of his finest poetry unquestionably written in very late old age.

We should notice that Hardy's poetic reputation has not yet been settled. From being comparatively neglected, he has gone to being the most important poet, in the eyes of one critic, of the last two hundred years. This is without doubt an over-valuation. It also calls into question what we mean when we use adjectives like 'great', 'most important' and 'major'. Such labels can reflect only a personal position or the position which is derived from a consensus view. In essence, written poetry (and other forms of print) are black marks on the page. We are able to read them only because our culture has equipped us to do so. Our culture also equips us with the techniques by which we can make an evaluation. The words themselves are open. Closure is visited upon them by these techniques, by our response, and if we are desperately unlucky, by the ways in which we are *told* to respond. That Hardy's reputation is in a state of transition gives the reader an almost unique possibility of arriving at a personal decision. Go to Hardy, read him, as you read make notes, 'This I like' and 'This I don't'. Try to make up your own mind. (Remember that Hardy was a musician – his poems should be read aloud, or you should listen to a trained reader reading them aloud.) And it is worth noting how modern his language is. There are, of course, deliberate archaisms, old-fashioned words which have been lost from contemporary English, but over and above that is the sound of a personal voice talking not writing. The language has a comfortable flow; only in the worst poems is it bent to accommodate rhyme and rhythm.

If we concede the personal nature of a great deal of Hardy's poetry this leads us back to his own life about which more may be necessary. The two volumes of biography which appeared in 1928 and 1930, apparently written by his second wife Florence, were in fact ghost-written by Hardy himself. They are not to be trusted. That he chose this method of publication suggests a desire for concealment which should arouse suspicion. The result was a construction, a shaping which, though not untruthful, was not what an unbiased reader would take to be a factual account. Modern readers are fortunate to have Robert Gittings' superb two volume biography which illuminates Hardy's life and adds personal meaning to the art.

Among the most important elements of that life were Hardy's first marriage and the huge number of poems – certainly the best poems of his career – which came about after his wife's death.

Hardy's nature was a passionate one and he had a powerful sexual drive which tormented him into old age. The torment was of two kinds. He fell in love readily, often with women who were younger, married, and (we are told) faithful, which made rejection certain, and indeed may have been what Hardy himself truly desired. But the torment was also present in Hardy's struggle to write about sex against the prevailing bourgeois values of his culture. Sexual themes are present from the early poems and led to the furious reception given to *Jude the Obscure*, the last novel he ever wrote.

What we know of that first marriage to Emma Gifford, whose family occupied a far higher social position than his own, was that it was happy in its beginning and bitter and angry at its end. Hardy's shyness concealed a nature capable of coldness and cruelty. Emma's distaste for her husband's pursuit of younger women turned to hatred, and led to an icy indifference on Hardy's part which lasted up until the moment of her dying.

Thereafter, however, followed a burst of poetry unique in twentieth-century literature. The poems are anguished revisitings of times and places in their courtship forty years before. These poems are Hardy's greatest achievement, and they are unquestionably among the finest in the language.

It is to these poems that every reader of Hardy returns. Their magnetism is built round a complex of love and loss, memory and guilt, pain and self-pity, beauty and regret, intermingled with something of delight. One is aware too that it is the act of writing which makes the experiences which they record bearable. Is what is happening in these poems an act of exorcism?

'At Castle Boterel' (really Bocastle, near St Juliot in Cornwall where Hardy first met Emma) mixes past and present holding them in tension. What is the mood of this poem? Ghosts move between the lines – not 'a girl' but 'a girlish form', a 'phantom figure'. Memory is its own supernatural domain, and the shadows which gather at the interface between what is and what might have been are forever alive in a vortex of disturbance.

The poem begins with the arrival at a junction. The physical detail is important because time, too, has its junctions, joinings and partings, points of decision. But the poet looks back, back down the road but also back into the past. The day is rainy (how often these poems of aroused memories have rain as their background), but the day which is at the poem's centre is dry. It is March – spring. They have been 'benighted' and they are walking beside the small carriage. The past has distanced them and Hardy now looks at himself and Emma almost as if they were other people, strangers, perhaps characters in a play with as much and as little significance. For the two lovers, however, and for their existence as symbols in a cosmic drama, their significance is eternal, one which the world of nature conspires in, perhaps even promotes. The two instants are alive (the instant of memory and the instant of the events which he is describing) with remembered potentials: roads taken, decisions made, which cannot be escaped or denied.

The geological record of the rocks that line the roadside reminds him of the fleeting nature of life and of its experiences. They also record, however, the moments Hardy describes, yet for the rocks, set against the record of mutability which they store, the event is less significant. Hardy and Emma 'passed' – a play on words in the sense that they were on the road, travelling, and also more tragically, that their lives were brief when set against the scale of things which the rocks record. The time lines in the poem are complex; the present, the hypothetical moment of experience, is not the moment at which Hardy wrote it, is not the moment at which we read it, is not the moment in which the distant lovers walked, is not the moment (whether real or imagined we cannot tell) in which Hardy drove the waggonette – although the present tense is persuasive. Far more real in the poem is the geological timescale which dwarfs everything, which is in a curious sense a consolation that Hardy offers. But it is unsatisfactory. The sense of the tragic, the inescapability not just of death but of the consequences of decisions taken, fill the poem to overflowing.

The person that was is no more than a phantom, an 'it' which shrinks and shrinks into an invisibility. Although we have been aware throughout the poem of the nature of its meaning, an active painful memory, the final verse brings us back to the present. It rushes in upon us like dark weather. The rain returns. The poet feels the onset of age, perhaps even a sense of his own death which the ghost has brought with it. This is a journey – of the body, certainly, perhaps of the imagination – which he will not take again. Although we can guess that this is no more than an attitude being struck, the last line of the poem carries with it a finality, perhaps even a deliberate switching off, which is agonising.

When we look at what might be called 'the telling' of the poem we are struck by its simplicity. The words move with a conversational flow which is characteristically modern. As well as the subtle rhythms we might notice the run-over lines, the alliteration, the techniques that invite the poem to be spoken.

'The Voice' too carries with it both the ghostly quality of a seance and the iciness which accompanies the appearance of a spirit.

Woman much missed, how you call to me, call to me
Saying that now you are not as you were,
When you had changed from the one who was all to
  me,
But as at first, when our day was fair.

The call echoes in the first line followed by a rapid and intensive flow of changing tenses that suggests in a brief compass the altercations, starts and endings which Hardy had had with his wife. But in the last verse we are recalled to the present and Hardy's faltering steps forward, and notice that the language throughout the poem suggests in its hesitations the turns of memory and the groping towards a final, definitive position which will be forever unattainable.

In the second verse the past becomes a vision. In the almost certainty of hearing her voice, he struggles to glimpse the woman wearing a summer gown as she had during the days of their courtship. Again we see the metaphor of climate and season being used to register inner states of feeling.

The words are exciting but the third verse declares a failure of vision, reality breaks in and the woman fades into unawareness. Loneliness and despair intrude as the call of the woman/the vision changes into something natural, the listless wind.

By the final verse the landscape is autumnal, the mood is desperate, winter is in the wind, and the mood is established and intensified through the length of the lines, which are short and painful. The images are without comfort, balanced around the one long line whose clotted stresses and alliteration suggest not only doubt but the forlornness of a climate which is of the heart.

How cheerful it is, then, to turn to the delicate mood of 'A Thunderstorm in Town' – the thunderstorm is again in the emotions as much as the elements, the sudden impulse to kiss the girl denied by the ending of the spell of bad weather – and by the speed with which she leaves the cab while Hardy is left with no more than the impulse!

These are, of course, only partial readings of complex poems. We might return and examine them from other perspectives. We might burrow even more deeply into Hardy's life to surround this text with others, with biographical detail and with our interpretations of them. The poems might lead us to consider what is the nature of poetry. All poems call to us from positions of intensified reality. Almost automatically we place them within a history, either of the age or of the writer, in a way which is not an immediate requirement for the appreciation of a novel. We might consider the nature of 'At Castle Boterel's 'reality': in what sense did the events being described here 'take place'? If we knew that the words represent a form of complex metaphor for an experience, that the rest of it, the waggonette and the drizzle were all fictions, would this affect our feelings about the poem? Such questions are crucial. If we say that the poem would be damaged by such a revelation, then quite clearly, 'our' poem has a form of spiritual existence which transcends the words in which it is written. We are, in a sense, treating it as a form of holy writ. But is this justified?

How, then, to sum up? Hardy is that most unusual of writers – both a 'major' poet and a 'major' novelist. With the exception of D. H. Lawrence, the canon of English literature does not contain another. Why there should be this distinction between the skills of the novelist and the poet need not detain us, although its implications are worth pondering. There is, however, that other peculiarity directly concerned with Hardy which is even more remarkable. He is, so far as most readers are concerned and despite the confidence of the statements in the commentaries above, a relatively unknown poet. He appears, of course, in anthologies, but these appearances are still erratic, both in their frequency and in the choice of poems represented.

The casual reader may well be initially repelled by the apparent simplicity of his subjects, or what might appear to be the laboured nature of the verse forms. Such a reader might well assume that Hardy is a minor figure who commands our attention due to the quantity of his production rather than its quality. But those critics who are poets have valued his poetry at the highest level and have themselves been affected by it. Philip Larkin, Ted Hughes and Peter Levi are outstanding examples. The ideas in his poetry are lucidly expressed. And these ideas are not old-fashioned or out of temper with the times in which we live. His concerns with a natural world which, though beautiful, contains savage forces regulating mankind as much as the other life forms, is one which our culture now endorses. These forces are often seen in the conflicts which arise between human law and human nature, and are seen at their worst in the damage done to life by unrestrained greed and mindless technological advance. But humanity was for Hardy no more than a mote in the huge ocean of time and space, in which the universe exists coldly indifferent to human ambitions. Beliefs of this sort sit uneasily with religious faith but, although he rejected most of the conventional Christian beliefs, he continued to have a firm adherence to Christian values. He loved church services and his works show a deep knowledge of the Bible. He did indeed continue as a church-goer and had something of a yearning for a time when there was the comfort of conviction. His politics were, for his day and class, radical, but outside the framework of party conventions; he believed passionately in the essential importance of the individual no matter how humble his birth or upbringing.

Hardy is a pivotal figure. He points forward and back. It is important to remember that very few of our so-called 'modern' ideas cannot be traced to the nineteenth century. Hardy's was an age of scientific and technological discovery and of inevitable wonderings about the place of humanity in the universe that was being revealed.

Such changes were not superficial. Their profound nature was decisive in forming the electric cultures of high-speed information, hygiene, control and centralisation which the West now takes for granted. Hardy's younger contemporary H. G. Wells looked to that future with an eagerness which was not untouched by pessimism. Hardy himself admired it but his deepest feelings turned him towards a vanished age of small, green fields, country lives, and country matters, whose languages reached back a thousand years to Old English but whose meanings are timeless.

2. W. B. Yeats
by
VICTOR ASHTON

The son of an artist, William Butler Yeats always tended towards the eccentric, dabbling in the 1890's in the occult, in oriental mysticism and spiritualism. In an attempt to found a national literature, he drew from Celtic mythology, creating both poetry and plays from this material. His highly romantic 'Celtic Twilight' poems were accompanied by the yearning love poems addresssed to Maud Gonne, a political revolutionary who entered his life in his middle twenties and whom he unsuccessfully pursued for the next fifteen years. As Maud Gonne herself said: 'Willie was so silly'.

Involved in the sidelines of the Irish Republican Brotherhood, chiefly, it is said, to impress Maud Gonne, he worked tirelessly to promote a cultural revival alongside the political emergence of Ireland as an independent country. He helped to establish and, for some years managed, the Abbey Theatre, writing many plays for the new dramatic movement. With his friend Lady Gregory, he encouraged many younger writers, assuming the role of the aristocratic patron of the arts, holding court especially in her mansionhouse in the West of Ireland.

The eccentricity of his behaviour in his younger days was matched, in his mature years, by the eccentricity of his thought. In his prose writing, especially in *A Vision*, published in 1926, he propounded weird and wonderful theories on the human personality, theories of history, culture and civilisation. A glance at some of the ideas expressed in 'The Phases of the Moon' and on the cyclical progression of history – the gyres – will show just how idiosyncratic he was.

But out of all this, he produced in his middle and old age magnificent poetry, centred on hard, firm symbolism derived from his 'system', as he called his theories. So, progressively, his status was recognised. In Ireland, he was made a Senator of the newly established Free State; he was recognised internationally by the award of the Nobel Prize in 1923. He confounded critics who constantly expected his inspiration to run out, by continuing to write powerful and profound poetry even in his seventies.

Yeats has the misfortune to be remembered best by what is probably his worst poem, 'The Lake Isle of Innisfree'. He was embarrassed by it all through his life and when, as a world famous writer, he was called on to do broadcast recitals of his work in the 1930's, he would introduce it with the ironic words: 'If you know anything at all about me, you will expect me to read this.'

It represents all that is worst in his early Celtic Twilight writing, with its romantic idea of the poet living the simple life, close to nature, meditating alone. It was written in London in 1890 as he thought of an island in Lough Gill in County Sligo. It is easy to criticise: some critics have taken an unholy delight in taking it apart, rib from rib, and this is done most entertainingly by Robert Graves in 'The Common Asphodel' so there seems little point in me analysing it into the ground.

What Yeats was experimenting with was the folksy romantic image, expressed in the rather artificial 'poetic' language which was later given the name 'Kiltartanese', after the village of Kiltartan in the West of Ireland, near where Yeats lived. This was the 'peasant' English such as was alleged to be spoken by the ordinary people, but elevated into a high-flown style. So in the poem there is much play made of 'the veils of the morning' and 'evening full of the linnet's wings' – all the pseudo-Celtic romanticism against which all right-thinking Irish people have long since turned.

In the use of language here, sound seems far more important than meaning, with the onomatopoeic 'live alone in the bee-loud glade' and the alliterative 'lake water lapping with low sounds by the shore'. The whole effect is an evocation of a melancholy, wistful tone as in 'I shall have some peace there, for peace comes dropping slow', something which the writer seeks to convince us is felt 'in the deep heart's core' – whatever that means! It is typical of a certain strand in Irish writing in the 1890's and at the turn of the century when Celtic mysticism was very popular with the British public. Even at the time it was ridiculed as artificial by many people in Ireland – 'the mist that does be on the bog', they said in mocking parody.

In his early collections, Yeats produced many poems working on Celtic myths and mysticism, such as 'The Stolen Child', 'The Host of the Air', 'The Song of Wandering Aengus', 'The Hosting of the Sidhe'. Yeats turned away from all this eventually in his collection significantly named *Responsibilities*, published in 1914, when he addressed himself with more realism to the actual world. In his little poem 'A Coat', he tells how he had 'embroidered' his poetry:

> I made my song a coat
> covered with embroideries
> out of old mythologies

and of how, seeing this imitated so much, he finds that a barer, plainer style is more effective for expressing what he had to say. Progressively throughout his career, his style became plainer, often taking on the directness of colloquial English.

Something of the melancholy romantic note is again struck in the early poem 'When You Are Old', which is a re-working of the sixteenth-century poem 'Quand vous serez bien vielle' by the French poet Ronsard. It is a love poem to Maud Gonne.

In its way, this particular poem is quite finely written, imagining the young girl become old woman, reading the love poetry which had immortalised her and remembering the one man who had loved, not just her beauty, but 'the pilgrim soul', the striving, questing part of her nature, the man who had recognised her as a tragic heroine. It seems to me that the weakest part of the poem is the last three lines, where Love (with a capital L of course) is personified as a lonely hermit who has fled from the world 'and hid his face amid a crowd of stars'. It sounds quite eloquent, until the reader asks more closely what it MEANS! Once again, it is a high-flown vagueness.

The poem is interesting however, in that it is an early example of his use of the personal in poetry. Yeats, throughout his writing career, made a kind of mythology, using people he had known as if they were heroic figures of universal significance. Maud Gonne features in many of the later, more mature poems as a kind of tragic, destructive heroine, like Helen of Troy. John MacBride, the man she married, features as the buffoon, the 'drunken, vainglorious lout' in 'Easter 1916', redeemed only by his courage in the face of danger.

In the same way, Major Robert Gregory, the Irish airman in 'An Irish Airman Foresees his Death' is Yeats's Renaissance-type hero, the soldier, scholar, horseman, artist, thinker, architect who was also athlete and man of action. In another poem, 'In Memory of Major Robert Gregory', Yeats called him 'our Sidney and our perfect man' – the complete man, like Sir Philip Sydney the Elizabethan, who also died heroically in battle. To Yeats, Gregory was the natural aristocrat. (He was the son of Yeats's great friend, Lady Gregory of Coole Park, with whom Yeats worked in managing the Abbey Theatre and encouraging the Irish Literary Movement.) He had not been conscripted to fight in the First World War; he had not gone through any sense of duty; he had not been swayed by the jingoism of the time – 'Nor law, nor duty bade me fight,/Nor public men, nor cheering crowds'. He had no sense of patriotism and no hatred of the enemy – 'Those that I fight I do not hate,/Those that I guard I do not love'. Only his own locality, the village of Kiltartan, meant anything to him as a 'country' with which he could identify, and he saw no reason to believe that his death could make any significant difference to the lives of the people there. All through his life, Yeats admired what, in his great poem 'The Tower' (probably the best of all his poems) he called 'The pride of people that were/bound neither to Cause nor to State'. His hero in this poem is one such: knowing he will die in action in the air, he goes, for the excitement of it, 'a lonely impulse of delight/Drove to this tumult in the clouds'.

Yeats had very little time for the poetry of Wilfred Owen, Sassoon and the other 'Trench' poets. He refused to include them in his Oxford Book of Verse, considering that 'passive suffering is not a theme for poetry – in all the great tragedies, tragedy is a joy to the man who dies'. Most people would consider this an eccentric view, but it is out of this attitude that this particular poem comes. Yeats's aristocratic hero, seeing the colourless futility of ordinary life, finds the exhilaration of danger as something to be sought after for its own sake. Having won the Military Cross and the Legion d'Honneur, Gregory was shot down in 1918.

The poem is well-wrought, with its compactness, its precision, its use of 'balance' – to use Yeats's own word. The voice of the tragic hero weighs up the possibilities of life and death and this comes across perfectly in the series of poised antitheses running through the poem.

'Easter, 1916' is of course, an elegy for those who were killed in the Easter Rising and especially for the sixteen leaders who were afterwards executed. The second section of the poem refers directly to Constance Markiewicz, Patrick Pearse, Thomas MacDonagh, and John MacBride in that order. More important than merely individualising those who were killed, Yeats is considering how following a cause with absolute, unswerving devotion changes a person's character. The key words 'transformed' and 'changed' are repeated often in the poem in a kind of chorus: 'All changed, changed utterly:/A terrible beauty is born'. The unusual juxtaposition of the two words 'terrible' and 'beauty' conveys Yeats's horror at what had happened, as well as his exhilaration at the way in which those involved had given their lives with an almost effortless heroism.

A change has been wrought in all those involved. The old 'casual' life described in the first section, with its dull routine of work, money-making and 'polite, meaningless' conversation (everything which Yeats had reviled in an earlier poem, 'September, 1913') has turned out modern-day tragic heroes. The idea excites the writer, but it also appals him, and violence was a subject which Yeats always viewed in this ambivalent way.

The most interesting part of the poem is the third section in which Yeats uses the image of the stone in the stream to contrast the single-minded, implacable, purposefulness of those involved in a cause, with those whose lives change 'minute by minute', as everything in nature does. Those who have 'one purpose alone' become set apart from the majority of people, are superior beings, in a way. But there is also a suggestion that there is something frightening about this, since it 'makes a stone of the heart' – taking away the changeable sensitivity which is natural in people and replacing it by the dogmatic rigidity which total devotion demands.

'The Second Coming' is in my opinion, a key poem of the twentieth century. Like all great poems, it is highly compact, condensing a wealth of statement into very small bounds. It expresses the violence which is so much a feature of the twentieth century. Written in 1919 against the background of the slaughter of the First World War, the upheaval of the 1917 Revolution in Russia, the localised viciousness of the Troubles in Ireland, it captures the spirit of the times superbly well. It is also a prophetic statement, for it prophesies the coming of 'some revelation', an apocalypse which will overthrow all existing order and which will bring the end of the values which had held civilisation together. Just a look at the image of the 'rough beast' which is likely to appear on the European scene gives a terrifyingly familiar sense of the Fascist monster which emerged in Europe in the 1920's and the 1930's. It would be wrong to say that the 'rough beast' *was* Hitler (at the time when the poem was written he had not been heard of), but Yeats's prophetic vision of the future and his sensitivity to his own times appear all the greater when we consider how he is able to nudge us into recognising it so many years later.

The poem's greatness however, derives from the fact that it is more than just a comment on the writer's own times. It relates the twentieth century to the context of history which had produced it. Yeats is taking the 'long view' back over the course of Western civilisation, showing the inevitable disintegration of it, as well as expressing his sense of the present and anticipating the future. It has in this way, a universality which is very uncommon in such doom-laden poems.

The poem opens with the image of a falcon released from the hand of the falconer, climbing up in a spiral into the air. The repetition of 'ing' – 'Turning and turning in the widening gyre' – gives a sense of the falcon sweeping round and round in a repeating circle which is constantly becoming wider and wider and therefore further away from the control of its master. The direct statement which follows points to the significance of this: everything established is falling into disorder; no longer can the 'centre' hold civilisation together. So the image of falcon and falconer reflects society or civilised man getting out of the control of the Christian values on which Western culture has been based. The 'gyre' or spiralling movement of the hawk into the air signifies the evolutionary development of history, with the hold on civilised values progressively weakening as society moves on in time.

The stabbing, abrupt forcefulness of the three statements in the third and fourth lines as well as the bitterly
contemptuous tone of 'mere' and 'loosed', prepares the
reader for the second great image of the poem, that of the
'blood-dimmed tide', the inevitable and irresistible wave
of violence which, like the tide itself, periodically moves
in and out, as it has twice done with catastrophic effect
in our own century. The 'ceremony of innocence', the
ordered, established way of life, society's institutions, accepted behaviour – these are destroyed. Yeats, with his
aristocratic pretensions, loved ceremony and saw in it the
essence of all civilisation. What he says about life in
Lissadell and Coole Park, the big houses which he visited
often in the West of Ireland, shows his approval of everything being formally ordered and ceremonious. This is
what he wishes for his own child in 'A Prayer for My
Daughter'. He writes about such ceremony again in
'Meditations in Time of Civil War' in the section called
'Ancestral Houses'. In that poem however, which was
written in the middle of the Civil War in Ireland when
many such houses were being burnt down, Yeats is
uneasily aware that just as the established things of civilisation tend to be destroyed by violence, it is also true
that they often *grow* out of violent upheaval in the first
place as conquerors build up 'the gentleness none there
had ever known'. So the word 'drowned' here is ambivalent, signifying destruction, but perhaps also suggesting some kind of purification. It is significant that it
is the liberal, decent people in any society who tend to
lose faith first – while the extremists trying to overthrow
them become triumphantly self-assured. The three-fold
antithesis of those last two lines in the opening section
starkly speaks for any society threatened by violence. In
a civilisation where the 'centre cannot hold', a drastic
change must take place.

So, the second part of the poem begins with two dramatic statements, looking forward to an apocalypse
which will change everything. A 'Second Coming' is expected, but it is the direct opposite of the first coming.

This time it will not be the gentle Christ, the Lamb of God, but, instead, the 'rough beast' who will come to take over. Instead of forgiveness, meekness and tolerance, the new leader here seems monstrously vicious, cruel and calculating. Instead of the vulnerability of the Lamb, there is the predatory strength of the 'lion body'. Its human intelligence, 'head of a man', looks on the world with a 'gaze blank and pitiless as the sun', ready to devour anything that comes against it.

The language associated with the coming of the new leader has connotations of fear, disturbance and upheaval: verbs like 'troubles', 'reel', 'slouches'; nouns like 'darkness' and 'nightmare' (suggesting the coming of the Dark Ages over again); adjectives like 'blank', 'pitiless', 'indignant' and 'rough'. These convey horror at the new arrival on the face of the earth. There is a helpless, dramatic quality about it all and the words 'its hour come round at last' suggest that the emergence of this monstrous new phenomenon is inevitable, something preordained in the cycle of history. The ending of the poem with a question rather than a statement, makes it all the more terrifying as something which is sure to happen but not yet recognised for what it is. 'Slouches' with all its suggestion of aggressive, heavy thuggery contrasts magnificently with 'Bethlehem' and its connections with the Gentle Saviour whose place is being challenged.

The poem asks some fundamental questions about history: about how civilisations are all temporary (Yeats said it often), how their values or 'centre' lose their grip and have to be replaced by opposing values, how a leader is always needed with a philosophy on which things can be based. It suggests that history is cyclical and that the turning points are always violent as the old order is destroyed and the new replaces it.

Another magnificent poem, the sonnet 'Leda and the Swan' also deals with this idea. In it Yeats uses the violent rape of Leda by Zeus in the form of a swan to dramatise the turning point in history where the Heroic Age was replaced by the Classical Age (just as the latter was in turn replaced through Western Civilisation 'by a rocking cradle' and Christian values). History in this poem has an almost god-like power over the helpless human being Leda, who is part of it. She is the agent of history conceiving and giving birth to Castor and Pollux, Helen and Clytemnestra. But she is also helplessly conceiving the future, since Helen and Clytemnestra were the destroyers of the old Heroic Age. Yeats asks the question: 'Did she put on his knowledge with his power?' Do human beings see the consequences of what they are involved in at such violent turning points? Do they really determine their own destinies, or are they perhaps only 'caught up' (he uses these words with weight in the poem) in an overwhelming and incomprehensible force which sweeps them along?

'A Prayer for My Daughter' was written in June 1919, some months after the birth of Yeats's first child, Anne. It is not, I think, one of his best poems, for there is too much obvious construction in it, especially with the 'key' to the poem at the end: 'Ceremony's a name for the rich horn,/And custom for the spreading laurel tree.' But it is an achievement as a whole in that it succeeds in doing what Yeats so often does, making public statement out of personal situation. The poem is set in the mediaeval tower which Yeats had bought at Ballylee and in which he and his family lived during the summer months each year. He meditates in the poem on the kind of world his young daughter will have to grow up in and what sort of person he wishes her to be, so that she might live happily and in harmony with others.

The poem opens powerfully with an Atlantic storm blowing ashore. The infant daughter is asleep, unaware of the violence of the elements outside. It is a clear but unobtrusive metaphor for the violence of the world at large, into which she will have to enter though she does not yet know it. The father does, however, and 'a great gloom' is in his mind at the thought, for he foresees 'in excited reverie' that upheaval and uncertainty are coming: the 'roof-levelling wind' which is blowing through the world will destroy, just as 'the blood-dimmed tide' in 'The Second Coming' would sweep away what was ordered and established.

In the face of this threat, he wishes that his daughter will grow up, not as the dynamic, politically committed, heart-breakingly beautiful heroine, such as Maud Gonne had been to him, but as a gentle, generous-spirited, spontaneous person whose nature will be able to find itself without being swayed by the 'intellectual hatred' which Yeats saw in the fanaticism of the stormy world at large. It is a turn round from his earlier romantic love of the destructive beauty that he had celebrated in a poem like 'No Second Troy'. Now he asks instead that his daughter should have 'heart revealing intimacy'. He sees, from experience, that 'to be choked with hate/May well be of evil chances chief.' The heroines such as Helen of Troy and Venus and Maud Gonne destroyed their own happiness as well as that of others. 'Because of her opinionated mind', Maud Gonne had married MacBride, whom Yeats dismisses contemptuously as 'an old bellows full of angry wind', and so embarked on a marriage which quickly broke up. The claim is that intellectual dogmatism quickly distorts judgement and makes a personality bitterly arrogant, so that happiness is lost.

In fact he suggest that the attitudes *within* a person can be more destructive than the violent threat of the stormy world outside: 'If there's no hatred in a mind/Assault and battery of the wind/Can never tear the linnet from the leaf.' The two central symbols, the Horn of Plenty or cornucopia and the 'spreading laurel tree' are perhaps too obviously presented. Happiness is to be found in what he calls 'ceremony', a courteous, ordered, responsible way of living – this is the 'rich horn' of civilised life. He asks that his child may 'live like some green laurel/Rooted in one dear perpetual place'; that she have a sense of belonging rather than be a rootless individual. The word 'radical' in the second last stanza means rooted and Yeats is suggesting that the only chance for the individual in an anarchic, threatening world is to find its own true self, growing from such sure foundations, or roots, as a tree grows in a natural way: 'The soul recovers radical innocence'.

In the opinion of many people this is a rather reactionary viewpoint. Yeats is contemptuously attacking the great political, ideological movements which characterise the twentieth century: 'arrogance and hatred are the wares/Peddled in the thoroughfares.' These words convey Yeats's disapproval of mass movements. They have the connotations of the cheap, shoddy, commercial world which he despised and to which he considered himself superior when he wrote of his own lineage as 'blood that has not passed through any huckster's loin.' He is proposing that the individual remain remote from such common involvement – it is a standpoint which derives from his aristocratic pretension. These are attitudes typical of his middle age when he had turned away from his earlier romanticism, becoming a family man, gaining real public recognition as a Nobel prizewinner and Senator of the Irish Free State, seeing himself in the aristocratic Anglo-Irish tradition of the eighteenth century as one of 'the people of Burke and of Grattan/who gave, though free to refuse.'

Yeats wrote his best poetry in his sixties and seventies, which is unusual. Yeats was increasingly aware that physical deterioration was, in his case, accompanied by creative brilliance such as he had never had in his youth.

Poem after poem in his later work deals with the themes of ageing and deterioration of the body and the search for an artistic expression which would immortalise human life. During this period, Yeats's wide and eccentric reading led him to seize on 'Byzantium – towards the end of the first Christian millenium' as a symbol to represent the eternal. Yeats had been impressed by the Byzantine mosaics dating from the fifth and sixth centuries, which he had seen at Ravenna, and saw in them the miracle of what the imaginative mind of man could achieve, creating something which would last, so defying the laws of nature. In his earlier poem 'Sailing to Byzantium', he contrasts 'whatever is begotten, born and dies', the 'dying generations', with the 'monuments of unageing intellect' which man's artistic creation leaves behind.

In these Byzantium poems Yeats is, in his way, explaining the function of art. In 'Byzantium' he contrasts the confused sensuality of natural life, 'the fury and the mire of human veins', with unchanging creations like the sixth-century dome of St. Sophia built by the Byzantines. The immortal art stands in contrast to mortal man: 'A starlit or a moonlit dome disdains/All that man is'. The word 'disdains' suggests that, to achieve the immortality of artistic creations, the imagination must reach beyond the immediacy of life, must 'purge' itself of its surroundings (the drunken soldiers, the prostitutes, the appetites and passions of life) and become, as it were, a soul released from the body 'the superhuman:/I call it death-in-life and life-in-death'. In 'changeless metal', the immortality seeking, creative soul of man can make an eternal artifice, symbolised here by the golden bird on the bough, such as in the mosaics, and this art will 'scorn aloud . . . common bird or petal/and all complexities of mire and blood'.

There is much more in the poem than is dealt with in this brief commentary: it is an experience just to read it, for it celebrates the whole atmosphere of Byzantium with its art and achievements, describing the Emperor's pavement, the mosaics in Constantine's forum and the workshops of the goldsmiths – nothing is redundant in the poem. The description of the purgatorial fires depicted in the mosaics signifies the refining of man's soul; the dolphins were Byzantine symbols associated with the conveying of the souls of men across the sea separating mortal life from immortal life.

Yeats has here made his own 'monument of unageing intellect', his creative imagination defying 'the dying animal' of the body in which he was caught.

Yeats is a major twentieth-century poet, perhaps the greatest twentieth-century poet in English. In an age when poetry had already become a minority taste, he sought to establish the poet as a public figure and, with his own dominant presence, he was instrumental in the launching of a cultural revival in a new small nation. Fascinating as an eccentric personality, his career is full of contradictions. In youth, his work was light-weight, but in old age he struck unexpected profundity. Out of rather crackpot theories on history and civilisation, he created poetry with a powerful wisdom. Adopting a reactionary stance, despising much that he saw in the twentieth century, he made himself the unrivalled spokesman of a revolutionary era.

3. War Poetry
by
ROBBIE ROBERTSON

We have all been on the battlefields of the world. They are endlessly portrayed on films, in novels, in history lessons at school, in advertising, in poetry, on the daily news broadcasts from which we readily turn away our eyes, in the horrifying scenarios with which we contemplate our society's future. War is a constant background to our lives and the symbols of war belong to no time and to every time: blood, iron, flags, noise, darkness; and with them the feelings and attitudes – fear, bravery, hatred, horror, pain, grief, and patriotism. The people of these places of the imagination and of reality are with us constantly – the wounded, the heroes, the ordinary soldiers and the generals.

War, indeed, is a constant background to human culture. It occurs so often that an independent observer would be forced to conclude that, far from being one of life's abberations, it belongs intrinsically to that culture and is inescapable.

The role of war in poetry is therefore substantial, its appearance regulated by cultural needs, by the individual perspectives of the poet, by the demands of the audience. The terms of its discourses are similarly established.

For one, war might be seen as a stage on which humans become heroes, their struggles breeding definitions of heroism and nobility as social models by which lesser beings might live, endure and die. Another might use war as a complex metaphor for the pains and perils of life itself, an amalgam of intractable forces against which the hero fights. For yet another war might be used as the basis for a critique of society, its blindness to individual needs, its brutality an indication of cultural poverty or social inequalities. War, too, has been used as an amplifier, or an intensifier, of other themes – love, for example – where its existence in the background adds a frisson of dread or pain to add meaning to the message which is arrayed in the foreground.

Because of the nature of war, and its position of centrality in our culture, the subject also adds a particular intensity to poetry which is itself an intense, hot medium – hot in the sense that it demands a more imaginative participation than does perhaps any other printed medium. War, too, whether in the background or the foreground, rouses strong emotions, and the combination of these subjects is the guarantee of passionate engagement by both the poet and his or her audience.

For us World War I has a particular fascination. It was the first modern war whose weaponry, coupled with obsolescent tactics, and battles lasting months, produced a scale of slaughter which is still horrific seventy years after the event.

Thus that war seems like an archetype, a universal symbol for all wars. And its details, since it was also the time when photography and cinema were themselves becoming defined art forms, have become part of our national consciousness through books, television and films. There is also the unshakable feeling that it was (unlike World War II) an unnecessary war fought for the territorial ambitions of a ruling class who proceeded to conduct it with a callous disregard for the lives or well-being of the combatants. This gives it a poignant quality that nests it (somehow the appropriate adverb is 'comfortably') in a vanished age. Finally, and most remarkably, it was the occasion of a great deal of highly successful poetry, some of whose propagandist power has survived virtually intact. Add to that the drama of lives snuffed out at the height of their creative achievements and one has a tragic dimension with a mordant appeal.

Three poets typify both in their lives and in their poetry the messages of that war: Wilfred Owen, Siegfried Sassoon and Isaac Rosenberg. Two died in the war, one survived; two are famous, one is not. One is conscious of a roulette wheel spinning. In Owen's well-known sen-

Wilfred Owen

tences: 'My subject is War, and the pity of War. The Poetry is in the pity.' Of that trio, Owen has received the most substantial recognition.

There were, of course, others. The early years of the war produced poets such as Rupert Brooke and Julian Grenfell whose poetry was of a different kind, a celebration of war, an enthusiasm for it which Owen was later to attack in 'Dulce et Decorum Est'. The origin of such attitudes is, however, a lot more complex than Owen suggests. It was not poets who preached it; it was a feature of a warlike and expansionist imperial power, whose scattered empire was sustained by sacrifice and aggression. Popular arts of the time – music hall songs, articles in newspapers, cheap poetry and equally cheap fiction – all celebrated the virtues of soldiering for one's country. Brooke and Grenfell articulated a national attitude, and one which transcended the notional restrictions of class. This can be seen clearly in the popularity of such poetry whose vast sales were sustained throughout the four-year period of the war and indeed beyond it. But already there were critics. In Arthur Graeme West's words:

God! how I hate you, you young cheerful men,
Whose pious poetry blossoms on your graves
As soon as you are in them.

There was also a more serious feeling that the poetry was over-valued and its sentiments cheap.

These feelings mounted as the war settled into bloody stalemate. And a new group of poets began to emerge – the three mentioned above, Owen, Sassoon and Rosenberg, also Hebert Read, Robert Graves and Edmund Blunden. To them should be added poets as diverse as Rudyard Kipling, Thomas Hardy and A. E. Housman. Wilfred Owen is, however, the poet who, it is generally agreed, best expressed not only the realism of conflict with its attendant human suffering, but also gave to his descriptions a depth of moral reality and compassion which help to establish a humane empathy for the soldiers of both sides, which moves his poetry onto a higher plain of spiritual significance. With his tone of genuine anger one has a poetry of extraordinary range and feeling.

Take for example, 'Anthem for Doomed Youth'. This extraordinary sonnet combines anger and elegy. Essentially it blends together the descriptions and feelings of a peacetime funeral with the strongly contrasted description of death in battle. In the octet, this contrast is at its most forceful, and there is a subtle inter-weaving of terms from that peacetime – 'passing-bells', 'orisons', 'prayers', 'bells' and 'choirs'. The mood is established in the first line when those who die are compared to cattle, and the onomatopoeic noises of the weaponry are compared ironically, to prayers, and this almost anti-religious note is sustained by the reference to the mournful sound 'of wailing shells' and the sounds of future requiems in their own localities. Reference to Britain bridges the two halves of the sonnet and permits entry into the sestet which is made up of a series of pictures each of which carries with it the aura of grief and concludes with a funeral image of sadness and isolation:

And each slow dusk a drawing-down of blinds.

This system of contrasts is one of the most basic principles not only of poetry but of all the arts. We may see it working in terms of subject in 'Strange Meeting'. Here in a dream the poet escaped out of battle down into some underworld carved from mythology. It is Hell and the dreamer, alive, confronts one who is dead. What the dead man says is built up out of a sequence of balances and contrasts: hopelessness with hope, grief with glee, 'The Pity of War, the pity war distilled', content with discontent, courage and mystery with wisdom and mastery, and so on. The ghost he meets is the man he killed. War is the enemy, not the warrior.

This is seen best of all in Owen's most famous poem, 'Dulce et Decorum Est.' The poem may be thought of as having two related sections. The first, of sixteen lines, paints an unforgettable picture of a gas attack. The 5.9's are gas shells which fall behind a group of battle-weary troops returning to safety behind the lines. The picture of the men, the picture of the battlefield, the colours made eerily ghost-like by the falling flares, is both photographic and a premonition. The gas attack has the immediacy of reality itself. The scrap of dialogue, the description of terrified excitement, the image of the man without a gas mask drowning in the green chlorine carries for us, as for Owen, a horror that cannot be forgotten. The repetition of 'drowning' the culminating image of these opening lines, is intensified by the words 'guttering, choking' and the image of a candle flickering and about to go out is matched by the sound of the words suggesting the sounds of a man gasping for oxygen.

The final twelve lines add the consequence and the moral. Only Rosenberg's 'Dead Man's Dump' contains a more graphic description of the reality of war. It is as though Owen were a war artist commissioned to record the event. But the imagination is not only visual, it is also auditory and the onomatopoeic qualities of the words, held together by anger and revulsion, should be noticed.

The anger, which in retrospect one can see developing throughout the poem, reaches its culmination in the quotation from Horace which asserts that 'it is sweet and fitting to die for one's native land.' The 'friend' who is accused of repeating such sentiments to children is probably a children's writer, Jessie Pope, who was at the time writing poetry which encouraged an unthinking attitude to war.

This poem was almost certainly written at Craiglockhart War Hospital, Edinburgh, and was mightily influenced by Owen's meeting there Robert Graves and Siegfried Sassoon. Sassoon was in the hospital for a rather curious reason. In July, 1917, he had published a letter which he had sent to his commanding officer 'as an act of wilful defiance of military authority, because I believe that the war is being deliberately prolonged by those who have the

Siegfried Sassoon

power to end it'. The letter went on to protest 'against the political errors and insincerities for which the fighting men are being sacrificed'. Sassoon was a hero, with a Military Cross and a reputation for fierce fighting which had earned him the nickname of Mad Jack. Publication of the letter caused a storm and there was a real danger that Sassoon would be sent to prison. Robert Graves acted promptly. He made representations both to the Army and to powerful figures with an influence on the Government. Everybody was anxious to hush the affair up and Sassoon, with Graves as his 'escort', was sent to Craiglockhart to recuperate from a wound which he had received three months before.

Sassoon brought out the best in Owen partly through encouragement and partly through example. His own poetry now, however, seems the lesser work, although the satire remains savagely effective.

What Sassoon was attacking was cant, the posturing of senior officers and the illusions which were common back home in Blighty. The attack on cant one can see clearly in 'Blighters' when Sassoon intrudes a harsh note of reality into a music hall performance of 'We're sure the Kaiser loves our dear old Tanks!' with a savage comment:

I'd like to see a Tank come down the stalls,
Lurching to rag-time tunes, or 'Home, sweet Home',
And there'd be no more jokes in Music-halls
To mock the riddled corpses round Bapaume.

Sassoon sends photographs with feelings, his poems have the flavour of high journalism, but they lack that moral passion which is Owen's. Nevertheless, they convey as powerful a feeling of horror and they have a political dimension which Owen's poetry lacks. Owen's principal weakness is that he tends to see the war as a dreadful accident, horrifying in its consequences yet one for which he does not, or cannot, apportion blame. Sassoon's social realism must be pleasing to us, but there can be little doubt that Owen is the greater poet. In 'Strange

Meeting' we notice the prophetic intensity with which he describes the future of Germany; his constant struggle with large issues, the existence of God and the problem of pacificism.

Owen learnt willingly and struggled for improvement. His death on 4th November, 1918, robbed the twentieth century of a major, creative influence. A week later, Owen's brother Harold, many thousands of miles away off the coast of Africa, returned to his cabin to find his brother already sitting there. The ghost did not speak but only smiled. This silence

> radiated a quality which made his presence with
> me undeniably right, and in no way out of the
> ordinary. I loved having him there: I could not,
> and did not want to try to understand how he had
> got there. I was content to accept him, that he was
> here with me was sufficient.

This was on Armistice Day. The ghost is with us yet, and the reality.

Isaac Rosenberg like Owen (and Brooke, Grenfell, Mackintosh, Sorley and others) was a poet killed in the war. He had also the misfortune to be entirely ignored. Like Owen his poems were unpublished in his lifetime, but twenty years later a collected edition was produced.

It is difficult to identify Rosenberg's quality in a few words. Part of his distinctive effect comes from his having been a private. He sees the world from the ranks and his topics reflect that: louse hunting, the heavy work of mules and carts, returning to camp. These topics are reported from inside the experience. Yet there is also a distinctively personal tone. He lacks the anger of the officers, Owen and Sassoon. There is indeed a note almost of resignation in his descriptions as he lets the horror speak for itself, but he does not fail to catch the occasional, optimistic beauty of the day or event, picking poppies, for example. In 'Returning, We Hear the Larks' the night is made splendid by the birds' song and yet

Death could drop from the dark
As easily as song —
But song only dropped,
Like a blind man's dreams on the sand
By dangerous tides,
Like a girl's dark hair for she dreams no ruin lies there,
Or her kisses where a serpent hides.

Although Rosenberg's quality as a poet (and his war poetry is only a tiny part of his writing) has not been given its due regard, one of his poems has been often anthologised – 'Dead Man's Dump'. This super-realist account of war from the viewpoint of the corpses has an icy quality which teeters on the edge of the merely loathsome.

They left this dead with the older dead,
Stretched at the cross roads.
Burnt black by strange decay,
Their sinister faces lie
The lid over each eye,
The grass and coloured clay
More motion have than they,
Joined to the great sunk silences.

The bodies are crushed or passed by the carts – even one just newly dead. There is a lack of regard for them, a departure from life's significance, which Rosenberg reports with a detachment counterbalanced by a sympathy of language and of emotion. That detachment might well be seen as the poem's subject. In war the individual has no value, men become callous, human values themselves become nothing. In a sense this detachment, lack of anger, reportage, points towards the future and towards the sort of poetry which was to emerge from World War II. But Rosenberg's voice is distinctive. The language, rich with biblical reference, is his own. The densely packed imagery, curious syntax, distinctive point of view, do not make for easy, or comfortable reading. 'Louse Hunting' is as grimly realist a poem as one could wish to read but behind it lurks, one readily imagines, a more awful meaning.

> See the gibbering shadows
> Mixed with the battled arms on the wall.
> See gargantuan hooked fingers
> Pluck in supreme flesh
> To smutch supreme littleness.

The British Poetry of World War II has received scant attention in schools. Its major figures, Alun Lewis, Keyes, Reed, are perceived as less important than the earlier poets whom we have been discussing. To some extent this is because of the nature of the poetry rather than its quality. Its lack of propagandist force gives it a personal emphasis whose quietness reduces its drama. The war was, in the view of many, a just one and there were no immediately recognisable targets against which to direct either anger or satire. The carnage, at least on the Western Front, was very much less. Both generals and politicians received considerable popular support. Film and the press were giving a more accurate picture of what the war was about than had the jingoistic effusions of the First World War. Civilians were themselves experiencing the horror of war at first hand in the Blitz. Perhaps, too, the scientific nature of the weaponry and the tactics reduced the passionate engagement with the topic of war itself. There is a distinctive lack of heroics, of dramatic statement in the poetry. The war as an ordinary affair, as business, is caught superbly in Henry Reed's 'Lessons of the War' (in particular Parts I and II, 'Naming of Parts' and 'Judging Distances') with their subtle contrasts and ironies.

This is the lower sling swivel. And this
Is the upper sling swivel, whose use you will see
When you are given your slings. And this is the piling
    swivel,
Which in your case you have not got. The branches
Hold in the gardens their silent, eloquent gestures,
    Which in our case we have not got.

These poems represent essentially an experiment with tones: the voices of the instructors, crisp, mechanical, insensitive, ungrammatical, and the contrast with the poet's voice, the poet's eye for significance, and the horrific distance which lies between.

Perhaps the most useful parallel, with the First World War's poets is offered by Keith Douglas's 'Vergissmeinnicht' (Forget-me-not), a poem whose subject matter is itself unforgettable. The picture of the enemy is the same as Owen's. The dead body of the German is accompanied by a fallen, 'dishonoured' photograph of his girlfriend, but the triple contrast between his soft, domestic, human engagement, the hardness and undecayed nature of the weapons, and the graphic description of the swollen, burst body belongs to a different age. The horror is directly gazed upon but is muted, the preferred interpretation is only fleetingly pointed up by language. Appropriately, perhaps, the poem has the stillness of a photograph. We read its messages with pity.

The poem which comes closest to the feeling of outrage which was the distinctive tone of the finest poetry of the First World War belongs to an American, Randall Jarrell in 'The Death of the Ball Turret Gunner'. This poem, all five lines of it, returns us to that lack of regard for man which was a preoccupation of Owen and Sassoon. Jarrell's last line 'When I died they washed me out of the turret with a hose' catches the feeling of insignificance. Yet Jarrell's true target is not the war and the inhumanity which it breeds, but the nature of modern society itself, its anomie, the way in which life has become translated into a brute existence.

War continues to be an obsession. Vietnam produced its stock of poems, but by far the most important strand of war poetry is concerned with the approaching nuclear conflict. Porter's 'Your Attention Please' defines not only the horror of that potentially arriving situation but the mechanical relationship to life which might allow it to happen. The robot voice giving instructions is the ultimate construct of dehumanisation, and that callous disregard for the human which links it to Sassoon. The tone is new. The enemy is not the bungling general, the incompetent politician. The enemy now, more terrifyingly, is seen as being within ourselves. The finger is pointing remorselessly at us. This is our future, we are to blame.

In Edwin Muir's 'The Horses' a similar apocalypse is described, an unwinding of the world over the seven days of destruction but at the end of that time the horses, a symbol of redemption and love, arrive to replace the machinery which, it is implied, caused the war. The poem now seems old-fashioned. In the landscapes which poetry offers in the latter half of this century, there is no redemption. War, should it burst upon us, will be a final act of lunacy and we will all be 'Joined to the great sunk silences'.

4. Wilfred Owen's 'Strange Meeting'
by
RONALD STEVENSON

(Ronald Stevenson, pianist, composer and musicologist, unlike the other contributors to this volume, is not and has not been a professional teacher of literature. In the short piece which follows, he offers his comments as a musician on Owen's 'Strange Meeting', emphasising the significance of sound in poetry and the links between poetry in our time and poetry of the past.)

Slow and quiet*
(*Lento e tranquillo*)
Recit.

TENOR SOLO

The form of the poem can be absorbed at a glance: a paragraph of forty-four lines, all of them long, except for a final, short, monosyllabic line. The reader's eye catches the word 'tunnel' in line two. The whole poem is a journey through a tunnel. That last, short line is like the opening at the tunnel's end.

Begin with one line. A verse was originally one line, not a stanza: it meant a ploughed furrow. Each line of Owen's poem is a trench through which we enter the dugout or tunnel of the poem.

We read a few lines and soon realise that they go in

* In 1961 Benjamin Britten composed his *War Requiem*, a setting for solo voices, chorus and orchestra of the *Missa pro Defunctis* and selections from poems by Wilfred Owen, including 'Strange Meeting'. The music illustration which heads this essay is from the vocal score. © Copyright 1962 by Boosey & Hawkes Music Publishers Ltd. Reprinted by permission of Boosey & Hawkes Music Publishers.

pairs – which are called couplets. This word derives from the French, meaning two pieces of iron riveted or hinged together. Each of Owen's couplets is like a hand-grenade: it explodes when the reader grasps its meaning.

Count the syllables of any line except the last. There are ten syllables to each line. Feel the rhythm: it goes short/long. The *iambus*. That Greek word meant a leg. The rhythm trudges like boot-shod feet through trench-mud. There are five stresses to a line: the iambic pentameter. Here Owen uses one of the oldest verse forms in English, invented by Chaucer and named the heroic couplet. Here is an example from Chaucer (fourteenth century):

Ănd thūs thĕ lōngĕ dāy ĭn fīght thĕy spēnd

Till, āt thĕ lāst, as ēverỹthĭng hăs ēnd . . .

The Scot, Blind Harry (fifteenth century), in his poem *The Wallace* and another Scot, Gavin Douglas (sixteenth century) in his translation of the *Aeneid*, continued the Chaucerian practice of the couplet, as did, of course, the eighteenth-century poet Pope.

With Owen, in the early twentieth century, the heroic couplet becomes an anti-heroic couplet. Notice the rhymes. They are not true rhymes. Real rhyme gives a sense of harmoniousness. Owen wants to convey the discord of war. He uses assonance, or half-rhyme. 'Escaped' half-rhymes with 'since scooped': 'groined' with 'groaned' and so on. It is to the ear what looking through a distorting mirror is to the eye. This assonance gives the poem a modern dissonance, just as much twentieth-century music is more dissonant than most earlier music.

Poetry and music share rhythm and sound. The rhythm of poetry is stressed by consonants. Poetry's melody or tune is heard in vowels. There are soft and hard consonants; closed or open, short or long vowels.

The sibilant, susurrous (hissing, whistling) 's' consonants in line 1 softly capture the dream or nightmare of escape from battle. Notice how the hard consonants of that word 'battle' are distant shell-thuds exploding in the dreamscape of words.

Notice the vowel sounds of line 2: 'Down some profound dull tunnel, long since scooped . . .' Subtract the consonants and the vowel sounds are –

ow – ugh – oh – ow – ugh – ugh – – – – – – oo!

Those are all the vowel sounds except the seventh to ninth. That succession of sounds is woven out of cries of pain. So we see – or rather hear – how the mood of the poem is suggested by the music of the words.

This analysis of the music of the poem – broken down into its constituent hard or soft consonants, and closed or open, short or long vowels – can be applied to the whole of this poem (or any other).

Observe, too, the fusion of image and sound in line 3: 'Through granites which titanic wars had groined'. There the very texture of the rock is suggested by the hard 'g' and 't' consonants.

James Joyce, a master of verbal music, ends his novel *Finnegans Wake* with the word 'the', without a full stop, wanting, as he said, the sound that gets nearest to silence. Apply this to the image of dead soldiers in line 5: 'Too fast in thought or death to be bestirred.'

The story of the poem is simple. The British soldier-poet has killed a German. He has a nightmare about it. He explores a tunnel. It is Hell. Its passages are strewn with recumbent ghosts. The poet recognises his victim and they talk. The German tells him what he might have done with his life. Most of all, he would have wished to live to tell the tale of war:

> For of my glee might many men have laughed
> And of my weeping something had been left,
> Which must die now. I mean the truth untold,
> The pity of war, the pity war distilled.

In lines 34 to 36 Owen employs allusion:

> Then, when much blood had clogged their chariot
>   wheels,
> I would go up and wash them from sweet wells,
> Even with truths that lie too deep for taint.

That last line echoes, alludes to one from Words-worth's 'Intimations of Immortality':

> To me the meanest flower that blows can give
> Thoughts that do often lie too deep for tears.

Allusion – one poet's use of the words of another, significantly changed – is a technique employed by poets particularly over the last hundred years. Ezra Pound in 1919 wrote,

> Go, dumb-born book,
> Tell her that sang me once that song of Lawes . . .

That is an allusion to a poem by Waller, set to music by Henry Lawes in the seventeenth century:

> Go, lovely rose,
> Tell her that wastes her time and me. . . .

So, line 39 of Owen's poem is problematic, unless we relate it to an incident in the passion of Christ:

> Foreheads of men have bled where no wounds were.

In dread, fear unto death, men sweat blood, as Christ did in the Garden of Gethsemene.
Line 40 alludes to the Christian ethic, or rather its betrayal in the murder (instead of love) of one's neighbour:

> I am the enemy you killed, my friend.

The irony encapsulates the futility of war that makes enemies out of friends. The laconicism of the last line is the only possible ending:

Let us sleep now.

Wilfred Owen was a realist. At a time when some others were belligerent jingoists, for him the adage about the glory of dying for one's country was 'the old lie'. His poetry was a warning, even more potent now than in 1914–18.

Owen died in action in the last week of World War I. He was twenty-five.

5. Robert Frost (1874–1963)

by
LESLEY WILLIAMS

With Vermont and Maine, New Hampshire is one of the wooded hilly states of north-east U.S.A. where the Appalachian Mountains reach the Canadian border – far from cosmopolitan cities like New York; and further from Chicago, the prairies and the Wild West; and even further still from the promised land of California.

In 'Mending Wall' we meet the poet in dialogue with a fellow farmer, his neighbour beyond the hill. He is 'all pine' whereas Frost (presumably the 'I' of the poem) is 'apple orchard'. Each spring they meet to repair the gaps in their boundary walls. Round this annual task Frost forges a poem full of wonder at the ways of nature and still greater wonder at the ways of human nature, in this instance the distance between one man and another. Where do the many gaps come from, he wonders:

No one has seen them made or heard them made,
But at spring mending-time we find them there.

Something there is that doesn't love a wall
That wants it down.

As the two farmers replace the stones, they keep the wall between them. To the poet, their work is

Oh, just another kind of outdoor game,
One on a side,

a game where the shapes of the stones are such that they have to use a spell to make them balance. The magic words are 'Stay where you are until our backs are turned!' His neighbour does not share Frost's lightheartedness and resists any suggestions that

There where it is we do not need the wall:
He is all pine and I am apple orchard,
My apple trees will never get across
And eat the cones under his pines, I tell him.

'Good fences make good neighbours,' the neighbour asserts. Frost concludes the poem with a reassertion of his neighbour's point of view, but casts doubt on its truth by having his apple farmer think aloud in between:

Why do they make good neighbours? Isn't it
Where there are cows? But here there are no cows.
Before I built a wall I'd ask to know
What I was walling in or walling out,
And to whom I was like to give offence.

Here in the use of walls we find a duality characteristic of Frost: an *actual* boundary wall is being mended and a *metaphorical* wall divides the menders. The communication barrier between the pine man and the apple man remains wide while the gaps in the actual wall between their woods are filled. Our final picture of the neighbour sets him apart from Frost and from us:

I see him there,
Bringing a stone grasped firmly by the top
In each hand, like an old-stone savage armed.
He moves in darkness as it seems to me,
Not of woods only and the shade of trees.

What this darkness is, is left unstated but is nevertheless evocative of the gulf that separates one human soul from another.

This sense of alone-ness is a central theme for Frost and is exemplified in a more personal way in 'Desert Places'. Neither a desolate, increasingly snowy landscape nor 'empty spaces between stars – on stars where no human race is' are to be compared with his own individual feeling of isolation:

> I have it in me so much nearer home
> To scare myself with my own desert places.

This later poem has none of the humorous tone of 'Mending Wall' with its speculation that elves may want the wall down or that spells may be needed to reset the 'loaves' and 'balls'. Both poems however, are similar in structure: a scene is initially created, a situation established; this then is developed to an ending which engages a response from us, the readers – perhaps we agree, perhaps we wonder. Where are my 'desert places'? 'Good fences make good neighbours.' Do they? Perhaps.

'Stopping by Woods on a Snowy Evening' is one of Frost's many poems which turn on a choice. The actuality of the 'lovely, dark, and deep' woods filling up with snow beside a frozen lake is set against an image of life being a journey, involving decisions and choices – irrevocable and not necessarily explicable. Contrary to the instinct of the little horse to keep going, Frost chooses to pause in the 'easy wind' and 'downy flake' to admire the 'woods fill up with snow'. He too moves on soon, despite the loveliness of the woods:

> The woods are lovely, dark, and deep,
> But I have promises to keep,
> And miles to go before I sleep,
> And miles to go before I sleep.

Repetition quietly endorses for us the necessity to move on. Time cannot be stopped or reversed. He must not be lured away from his human duties by the intriguing mysteriousness of these deep woods.

In 'The Road Not Taken' a choice of direction is offered. In a 'yellow wood' grassy paths diverge, each carpeted with 'leaves no step had trodden black'. Which way to go? He expresses sorrow that he could not travel both roads and be 'one traveller'. He 'took the other' saying 'Oh, I kept the first for another day!' Acceptance, however, of the finality of his choice ends the poem:

Two roads diverged in a wood, and I –
I took the one less travelled by,
And that has made all the difference.

The individuality of his choice is highlighted by the repetition and rhyming on the 'I' at the end of the third last line.

A less down to earth 'choices' poem is entitled 'Fire and Ice':

Some say the world will end in fire,
Some say in ice.
From what I've tasted of desire
I hold with those who favour fire.
But if it had to perish twice,
I think I know enough of hate
To say that for destruction ice
Is also great
And would suffice.

Frost as ever the master of caution and guarded statement: ('some say', 'I hold', 'but if', 'I think' I know') leaves the response open to the reader. What do we hold? Would ice suffice? Do we favour fire? Will the world end? Frost is reticent about his own choices and resistant to choosing for others. Hardly surprising in such a context. Who would be so bold to make categorical assertions about the end of the world? Even at mundane level he avoids being driven into a decision. At the end of a long poem celebrating New Hampshire as an ideal place to live, he writes:

> Well, if I have to choose one or the other,
> I choose to be a plain New Hampshire farmer
> With an income in cash of say a thousand
> (From say a publisher in New York City).
> It's restful to arrive at a decision,
> And restful just to think about New Hampshire.

One further line, the last, withdraws the comfort and assurance of this decision. It is:

> At present I am living in Vermont.

I like his open-enedness and rejection of absolutes.

From the limited use of dialogue in 'Mending Wall' Frost has created more ambitious dialogue-cum-narratives which explore 'walls' between people. Favourites of mine are 'Home Burial', 'The Death of the Hired Man', 'The Code', and 'A Hundred Collars'. This last poem is closest in tone to 'Mending Wall' with a half in fun, half in earnest portrayal of strange room-mates. A wall of snobbery and refinement divides Dr Magoon, a teacher, from Lafe (Lafeyette), a chatty itinerant agent. When Lafe learns that the doctor's collar size is 14, he wants to give him a present of more than a hundred collars which are now too small for his own size 18 neck. Dr Magoon is horribly embarrassed:

> Though a great scholar, he's a democrat,
> If not at heart, at least on principle.

Their conversation reveals how difficult the educated man finds coping with the easy friendliness of the un-sophisticated Lafe. The other dialogues are wholly serious in tone. Both 'Home Burial' and 'The Death of the

Hired Man' examine the emotional distance between a young wife and husband faced with death and bereavement. In 'The Code' a hired man enlightens 'the town-bred farmer' about how to treat his workers respectfully:

> Don't let it bother you. You've found out something.
> The hand that knows his business won't be told
> To do work better or faster – those two things.
> I'm as particular as anyone:
> Most likely I'd have served you just the same.
> But I know you don't understand our ways.

Thus Frost engages his reader in opposed points of view and inevitably to the question: am I able to understand my friends, relations, colleagues, fellowmen, myself? The dialogue form is especially appropriate for exploring themes involving gulfs in communication, but length usually prevents their inclusion in anthologies.

Frost is also interested in the wider question of where we stand in time and eternity, a question which underlies 'Neither out Far nor in Deep'. This poem is unusual by the absence of an expressed first person pronoun, but we sense Frost's observer stance nonetheless. He notices that people on the beach 'turn their back on the land' and 'look at the sea all day'. They are not deterred by the fact that the land may offer more variety of scene and incident, nor that 'they cannot look out far' nor 'look in deep'. When, asks the poet, 'was that ever a bar/To any watch they keep?' The simplicity of word choice, of alternating rhymes, of easy syntax, suits his sense of the incomprehensible mysteries of creation and of our immortal human longings.

More often than the sea, Frost uses stars to portray the dimension beyond the here and now. A good example of this is one of his very last poems in which he apostrophises a star, 'the fairest one in sight':

> Say something to us we can learn
> By heart and when alone repeat.

For Frost, however, man's feet are always firmly on the ground, rooted in the good earth. 'Birches' treats this theme.

Birches

When I see birches bend to left and right
Across the lines of straighter darker trees,
I like to think some boy's been swinging them.
But swinging doesn't bend them down to stay
As ice-storms do. Often you must have seen them
Loaded with ice a sunny winter morning
After a rain. They click upon themselves
As the breeze rises, and turn many-coloured
As the stir cracks and crazes their enamel.
Soon the sun's warmth makes them shed crystal shells
Shattering and avalanching on the snow-crust –
Such heaps of broken glass to sweep away
You'd think the inner dome of heaven had fallen.
They are dragged to the withered bracken by the load
And they seem not to break; though once they are
       bowed
So low for long, they never right themselves:
You may see their trunks arching in the woods
Years afterwards, trailing their leaves on the ground
Like girls on hands and knees that throw their hair
Before them over their heads to dry in the sun.
But I was going to say when Truth broke in
With all her matter-of-fact about the ice-storm
I should prefer to have some boy bend them
As he went out and in to fetch the cows –
Some boy too far from town to learn baseball,
Whose only play was what he found himself,
Summer or winter, and could play alone.
One by one he subdued his father's trees
By riding them down over and over again
Until he took the stiffness out of them,
And not one but hung limp, not one was left

For him to conquer. He learned all there was
To learn about not launching out too soon
And so not carrying the tree away
Clear to the ground. He always kept his poise
To the top branches, climbing carefully
With the same pains you use to fill a cup
Up to the brim and even above the brim.
Then he flung outward, feet first, with a swish,
Kicking his way down through the air to the ground.
So was I once myself a swinger of birches.
And so I dream of going back to be.
It's when I'm weary of considerations,
And life is too much like a pathless wood
Where your face burns and tickles with the cobwebs
Broken across it, and one eye is weeping
From a twig's having lashed across it open.
I'd like to get away from earth awhile
And then come back to it and begin over.
May no fate wilfully misunderstand me
And half grant what I wish and snatch me away
Not to return. Earth's the right place for love:
I don't know where it's likely to go better.
I'd like to go by climbing a birch tree,
And climb black branches up a snow-white trunk
Toward heaven, till the tree could bear no more,
But dipped its top and set me down again.
That would be good both going and coming back.
One could do worse than be a swinger of birches.

Frost's own comment that a poem 'begins in delight and
ends in wisdom' fits 'Birches' exactly. From the opening,
delightful, scene of the birches bent 'to left and
right/Across the lines of straighter darker trees' Frost goes
on to picture the birches for us in more detail, 'Often you
must have seen them. . .' Listen to the sounds of the
thawing ice, clicking, cracking, crazing, shattering and
avalanching. Yet the fairly matter-of-fact explanation for
the bending of the trees, the ice-storm, does not satisfy
Frost. He returns to his earlier speculation that a boy had

something to do with the bending of the branches, 'I like to think some boy's been swinging them.' Frost delights in his imaginative explanation of the swinger and lets us share his admiration for the boy's technique and poise. The alliteration points the vigour and fluidity of the movement. Frost then extends the range of his vision,

> So was I once myself a swinger of birches.
> And so I dream of going back to be.

Swinging on birches becomes an image of carefree, happy times, something to be dreamed of. The poet, however, is no escapist. Witness his thoughts on going to heaven. While he would 'like to get away from earth awhile' he does not wish to be snatched away 'Not to return'. What he knows he wisely values and will not willingly forfeit.

> Earth's the right place for love:
> I don't know where it's likely to go better.

Frost has lots of time for this world of ours; his acute sensitivity to his environment shines through the sonnet 'Design'.

> I found a dimpled spider, fat and white,
> On a white heal-all, holding up a moth
> Like a white piece of rigid satin cloth –
> Assorted characters of death and blight
> Mixed ready to begin the morning right,
> Like the ingredients of a witches' broth –
> A snow-drop spider, a flower like a froth,
> And dead wings carried like a paper kite.

> What had that flower to do with being white,
> The wayside blue and innocent heal-all?
> What brought the kindred spider to that height,
> Then steered the white moth thither in the night?
> What but design of darkness to appal –
> If design govern in a thing so small.

A spider on a wild flower, odd in its whiteness being normally blue: why are both white? Why together at all? Chance or design? This whiteness may be a conspiracy against darkness. The final line is characteristically conditional: 'If design govern' such matters. I incline to the opinion that for Frost design does govern things large and small. His poetry expresses for me an optimism, a deeply rooted confidence in humanity and some sense of a fundamentally beneficent creative force. Despite the darkness of the world, its walls and barriers; despite the difficulty of choosing a star, in the end Frost stands as a poet conveying an abiding sense of wonder and delight in the planet Earth and its inhabitants. He has time for people.

Join this friendly and unassuming man by the 'stone wall' where he has time to talk. The conversation will not be one-sided.

A Time to Talk

When a friend calls to me from the road
And slows his horse to a meaning walk,
I don't stand still and look around
On all the hills I haven't hoed,
And shout from where I am 'What is it?'
No, not as there is a time to talk.
I thrust my hoe in the mellow ground,
Blade-end up and five feet tall,
And plod: I go up to the stone wall
For a friendly visit.

6. William Carlos Williams
by
EDWIN MORGAN

When you read a poem by William Carlos Williams, you are probably struck by two things: the subject of the poem tends to be down-to-earth and everyday, and the language of the poem tends to be unusually direct, often quite like speech itself. This sometimes makes his poetry look 'unpoetic', if you come to it with certain expectations about poetry as a high art, dealing with the highest things. It took quite a while for Williams's reputation to be established in his own country (America), and he is still less well-known in Britain than he should be. What makes his work so valuable is that when he is at his best he can prove to you, that his approach through ordinary subjects and direct speech can produce poetry of great quality, a very human poetry that digs into our basic concerns of life and death and love.

Williams was a doctor, working for most of his long life as a general practitioner in Rutherford, New Jersey, a small suburban borough in the unlovely north of that state, not very far from New York. He did not feel that this busy, time-consuming vocation was a hindrance to his work as a poet (though inevitably there were moments when he chafed at the bit), and in fact he believed it actually helped him. It is interesting to consider how and why this should be so. Looking back over his life in his *Autobiography* (1951), he wrote:

> As a writer I have never felt that medicine
> interfered with me but rather that it was my very
> food and drink, the very thing which made it
> possible for me to write. Was I not interested in
> man? There the thing was, right in front of me.

As a doctor living for many years in a small community,

he got to know a great variety of people, and had a strong sense of identity with that community, knowing its problems, its weaknesses, its virtues, and its hopes. This identification gave him glimpses of what in his autobiography he calls 'the underground stream' which suddenly comes near the surface and fills him with 'intense excitement' – it is the deep hidden life of the community which shows itself, in moments, through the individuals he knows as patients and friends, 'some secret twist of a whole community's pathetic way of thought'. It is his job, as a doctor, to *listen* to the often inarticulate patient trying to tell him about some pain or fear or anxiety, and out of that listening the poem begins to emerge:

> We begin to see that the underlying meaning of all
> they want to tell us and have always failed to
> communicate is the poem, the poem which their
> lives are being lived to realize.

It is not surprising therefore that Williams has several poems where he addresses 'my townspeople' in a directly immediate voice. In one he reminds them that love is cleansing and precious – like poetry. In another he warns them that he could easily leave them to their own devices and go to live 'beyond in the great world' – only he won't. And in 'Tract', which is the best of his poems of this kind, he harangues them on how to conduct a funeral. Why 'tract'? A tract is a pamphlet or leaflet on some moral, religious, or political subject, and it is usually hard-hitting because it is so short: it has to get its message across in a few pages, or even on a single sheet. Williams's tract is aimed at educating his townsfolk out of any wrong ideas they may have – probably do have! – about how a funeral procession should be ordered. He cajoles them, flatters them, attacks them, instructs them, mocks them, sympathizes with them, in an extraordinary succession of quick thoughts and feelings expressed in lines of widely varying length, full of dashes and exclamation-marks. The vehemence of his tract shows in the peppered expletives: 'For Christ's sake', 'My God', 'God knows what', 'For heaven's sake', 'damn him', 'Hell take curtains!' He boldly uses humour – black humour if you like – in asking whether the dead man wants a glass hearse to look out from, or in recommending the mourners to walk behind 'seventh class', or in reminding them sardonically that 'it will be money in your pockets' if they follow his advice – they'll save funeral expenses as well as preserve a proper simple dignity.

It has been said that death is the great taboo subject today, as sex was in Victorian times. If there is any truth in this, Williams's poem is doing its best to counteract the trend. A funeral is about a dead person, a neighbour or friend or relative who was alive a few days before; so don't try to gloss over or prettify or conceal the hard fact with flowers and glass and upholstery and curtains and top hats. 'Or do you think you can shut grief in?' Some might object that all the conventional trappings of a funeral are perfectly decent and respectful. But Williams will have none of it. Once you start along that road, he would argue, you are well on the way to comfortable crematoriums with soft music and mechanically-vanishing coffins, where any cry of grief would be regarded as being in decidedly bad taste. (Evelyn Waugh's novel, *The Loved One*, is recommended reading!)

And just as the doctor-poet wants us to keep an awareness of the stark reality of death – a theme he returns to in the bitter but expressive poem 'Death' – so also he celebrates the thrust of life, and again does it in a very basic way, in many of his poems, ranging over a broad spectrum of human and animal life, and even the life of plants, minerals, and objects. He is in general an optimistic poet, and enjoys particularly the theme of survival, of overcoming difficulties, of coming through, of asserting one's nature and one's spirit. 'The Sparrow' does this with the most ordinary and widespread of birds, praising its 'small size, keen eyes, serviceable beak and general truculence'.

> The way he swipes his beak
> > across a plank
> to clean it,
> > > is decisive.

And the bird's epitaph is: 'I did my best.' The well-chosen word 'swipes' brings out Williams's delight and gusto in observing and entering into the sparrow's straightforward way of getting on with the job.

The sparrow is regarded as a highly successful species. What about man? Can he be praised for any of the same reasons? Consider 'Dedication for a Plot of Ground', a poem about Williams's English grandmother. Emily Dickinson Wellcome, not unlike the sparrow, fights for survival with notable determination. She has such a strong character that the speaker still feels her 'living presence' as he dedicates the plot of ground. The poem enacts the troubles and triumphs of her life, its amazing twists and turns, by being almost entirely one long sentence, and the sentence marches along on the verbs which describe how the woman went through her experiences: 'lost', 'was driven', 'ran adrift', 'lost', 'lived hard', 'lost', 'lost', 'seized', 'fought', 'defended', 'grubbed', 'domineered', 'blackguarded', 'attained'. Someone who won't give in, even when the odds seem stacked impossibly against her – that's what the poet admires. The almost brutal warning at the end drives home the point:

> If you can bring nothing to this place
> but your carcass, keep out.

As in Arthur Miller's play, *Death of a Salesman*, the meaning is that 'attention must be paid', to such people, to such lives. It is a part of the democratic and individualistic aspect of the American genius.

So far, I have emphasised the sense of a voice in Williams's poetry, the feeling of a man standing in the poem and addressing a reader or an audience. But in one of the most famous of his poems there is something different, an emphasis on eye more than ear. 'The Red Wheelbarrow' is a very short piece, but a lot has been written about it by critics and interpreters. Why should this be? And what should we make of it? At first sight there may seem to be no great problem. The poem makes a clear statement and presents a clear picture. It is a pleasant picture, such as you might find on a calendar. However, although it is pleasant enough, you soon begin to wonder why this little scene of wheelbarrow and chickens in somebody's back yard should be such that 'so much depends upon' it. The statement begins to seem extravagant, perhaps sentimental. The Scottish term 'kailyard' looms in the wings: something agreeably small-scale, local, cosy, escapist. But if you continue to look at it, and think about it, that idea will not really hold. The language is too precise, too 'hard-edged' as a painter would say, and the words are placed too carefully for us to see this as merely a poem of rural sentiment. The wheelbarrow, which is the centre of interest, is not only a startling red in colour but glitters after a shower of rain: it is 'glazed' as a work of art, a piece of pottery or porcelain, might be glazed. It stands out, fresh eye-catching, both perfectly real and ordinary and man-made, yet at the same time it is a kind of vision, a revelation. The visual appeal of the poem is strong, and we know that Williams was much interested in painting, had artist friends, and grew up in the early years of the century when modern art began to make its impact on America. The measured movement of the poem, its numerical pattern not only of words but even of syllables (you should count them!), its separation of wheel/barrow and rain/water, all show effects that are aimed at the reader's eye and *inner* ear; if the poem is read aloud, many of these effects are lost. So there you have another kind of poetry, and one that in some ways leads on to the 'visual'or 'concrete' poetry of more recent times.

'No ideas but in things' was a favourite slogan of Williams's. The thing might be a wheelbarrow, a sycamore tree, a rock plant, a cod-head, a yacht, a fire-engine, a cat in a flower-pot. It was the 'real thing' that was to come first, the actuality, the hard fact. Out of this were to emerge the poetry, the ideas, the thoughts and suggestions. But what if the starting-point, the 'thing' was itself a work of art, a painting? How 'real' is a painting? Williams felt a certain kinship with the Flemish artist Brueghel (Pieter Brueghel the Elder, c.1525–1569), who excelled in painting realistic scenes of peasant life, both in work and play, sometimes moving towards pure landscape, sometimes moralising a fable or parable or proverb. The paintings are solidly 'real', and one can see why they would appeal to the poet who wrote a whole sequence of poems based on individual pictures. The poems pick out what he sees as the essential details, obviously leaving out a great deal but also adding whatever it is that words can add to colour, shape, and texture. But why do it at all? The Brueghel paintings are acknowledged masterpieces which don't need a writer to rescue them from neglect! Well, perhaps the eye of a sympathetic poet sees something, points out something, isolates something that otherwise we might miss.

In 'The Hunters in the Snow' he ends surprisingly with a reference to perhaps the least obvious feature of the painting, 'a winter-struck bush' in the middle of the foreground edge. He does not tell us why this is important – for the composition? as a symbol of life struggling to endure a bleak time? We have to guess. In 'The Parable of the Blind', where the picture of six blind beggars stumbling towards a ditch is based on *Matthew 15.xiv*, 'If one blind man guides another, they will both fall in the ditch', Williams adds pity for the wretched beggars with their handful of possessions, but at the same time ends his poem on a mocking, condemnatory note which is more in the spirit of the parable:

> stick in
> hand triumphant to disaster.

Is this confusing, do you think, or can you bring the two

attitudes together? Notice one characteristic detail: the painting, he says, is 'without a red', and all the grimmer for that; unlike his own word-picture of the wheelbarrow, where the red shines out in joy and assertiveness. You will often find that much of an author's work begins to mean more, when you see how one of his poems throws light on another.

The American poet Robert Lowell, a generation younger than Williams, wrote of him: 'It's as if no poet except Williams had really seen America or heard its language. Or rather, he sees and hears what we all see and hear and what is most obvious, but no one else has found this a help or an inspiration.' That seems a very fair summing-up.

7. John Betjeman
by
JEFFREY ALDRIDGE

In this century of constant battle with various bureaucracies, Betjeman's voice sounds clearly for smaller forces: those of quiet ordinariness; of landscapes and townscapes that complement rather than contradict each other; of a simple Christianity, with all its fears and doubts, and against the 'progressive' cynicism of more 'advanced' ideas. With all these, often setting up a fascinating counterpoint to his 'message', there is a distinctive humour and wit, a precise yet compassionate satire.

He is easy to dismiss as a mildly amusing but essentially minor figure. Many have thus dismissed him but they should be careful. Both Philip Larkin and W. H. Auden have reckoned Betjeman among the most important of twentieth-century poets; and it is a brave person who rejects their estimation without, at least, a careful consideration of Betjeman's work.

But at first glance it is easy to underestimate. In an age which has prized, variously, obscurity and intellectualism, stridency and vigour, hip-ness, concrete poetry and the freest of free verse, Betjeman's poetry looks distinctly odd. It is, by and large, easy to understand and written in a straightforward way. His favourite verse-forms are like those of hymns, his subject-matter is generally familiar – or, at least, not too out-of-the-way. He is easy to parody. Yet he is also an original – nobody before him had written verse quite like his.

> Gaily into Ruislip Gardens
>   Runs the red electric train,
> With a thousand Ta's and Pardon's
>   Daintily alights Elaine;
> Hurries down the concrete station
> With a frown of concentration,
> Out into the outskirt's edges
> Where a few surviving hedges
> Keep alive our lost Elysium – rural Middlesex again.
>
> Well cut Windsmoor flapping lightly,
>   Jacqmar scarf of mauve and green
> Hiding hair which, Friday nightly,
>   Delicately drowns in Drene;
> Fair Elaine the bobby-soxer,
> Fresh-complexioned with Innoxa,
> Gains the garden – father's hobby –
> Hangs her Windsmoor in the lobby,
> Settles down to sandwich supper and the television
>   screen.

Note the precision of detail here, even though we are given no physical description of Elaine. The Windsmoor coat and Jacqmar scarf show that she is well-dressed, if not in *haute-couture*. The only words she speaks say something of her social background: would it have been the same if she had said, 'Would you excuse me please?' instead of 'Ta' and 'Pardon'? Just two words – 'Father's hobby' – are needed to conjure up a neat, small suburban garden. The sandwich supper and the television, with the important words 'Settles down', tell us all we need to know about her after-work life. What is portrayed here, then, is a typical young woman from the suburbs, smart but not pretentious, content with her comfortable, respectable home life.

But what is the poet's attitude towards Elaine? Is it a satirical portrait? Or is it affectionate? The answer to both those questions is, I think, yes. It is this dual vision, one of affectionate satire, that gives much of Betjeman's poetry its unique quality.

The poem from which the above is taken is called 'Middlesex'. Elaine, her household and all they stand for, represent the area as Betjeman sees it in the second half of the twentieth century. The second half of the poem switches focus, back to the Middlesex Betjeman knew as a child.

> Gentle Brent, I used to know you
>   Wandering Wembley-wards at will,
> Now what change your waters show you
>   In the meadowlands you fill!
> Recollect the elm-trees misty
> And the footpaths climbing twisty
> Under cedar-shaded palings,
> Low laburnum-leaned-on railings,
> Out of Northolt on and upward to the heights of
>   Harrow hill.
>
> Parish of enormous hayfields
>   Perivale stood all alone,
> And from Greenford scent of mayfields
>   Most enticingly was blown
> Over market gardens tidy,
> Taverns for the *bona fide*,
> Cockney anglers, cockney shooters,
> Murray Poshes, Lupin Pooters
> Long in Kensal Green and Highgate silent under soot
>   and stone.

The mood is obviously different from that of the first half of the poem; it is now gently elegiac. The world has changed, at least in this corner. The semi-rural area has become just another part of the huge suburban sprawl. The cockney anglers and shooters who travelled out to Middlesex to pursue their sports are long dead 'in Kensal Green and Highgate' (cemeteries); the sports themselves can no longer be practised there. (Murray Posh and Lupin Pooter appear in George and Weedon Grossmith's splendid *Diary of a Nobody*, first published in 1892.)

The present is contrasted with the past, and does not come out too well. But it is important to recognise that this is not simply a nostalgia on Betjeman's part for things gone, nor is it a huge outburst against the desecration of a major beauty spot; by no stretch of the imagination could Middlesex be described as that. Betjeman's concerns are both larger and smaller. Like any sane person, he would rage against a proposal to build, say, half a million houses on stilts along both shores of Loch Lomond or series of office blocks around Stonehenge. Here and elsewhere, it is the undramatic but quietly useful areas of countryside that he is pleading for; they need our concern and husbandry too, since it is all too easy to let the 'planners' intrude on these (as they have, and still do). Eventually there would be precious little left.

Cambridge, I fear, is living in the past.
She needs more factories, not useless things
Like that great chapel which they keep at King's.
As for remote East Anglia, he who searches
Finds only thatch and vast, redundant churches.
But that's the dark side. I can safely say
A beauteous England's really on the way.
Already our hotels are pretty good
For those who're fond of very simple food –
Cod and two veg., free pepper, salt and mustard,
Followed by nice hard plums and lumpy custard,
A pint of bitter for one-and-four,
Then coffee in the lounge a shilling more.
In a few years this country will be looking
As uniform and tasty as its cooking.

That is but a small part of the philistine outpourings of 'The Town Clerk's Views'. There is no affection behind that particular satire. In this poem, and in two earlier ones, 'The Planster's Vision' and 'Slough', Betjeman allows no charity to temper his bile. And his targets are the same in all three: the soulless, 'planned' architectural projects that have sprung up since the 1920s, and those people who have conceived them. These last are attacked not simply because they planned and brought to fruition huge areas of similar, and uninspiring, buildings but, more importantly, because they dared to think that they could plan other people's lives, their welfare, their happiness.

> I have a Vision of The Future, chum,
>   The workers' flats in fields of soya beans
>   Tower up like silver pencils, score on score:
> And Surging Millions hear the Challenge come
>   From microphones in communal canteens
>   'No Right! No Wrong! All's perfect, evermore.'
>   *'The Planster's Vision'*

Once again, the words are carefully chosen to sharpen the attack. The use of the word 'chum' gives no sense of friendship or comradeship; it is more aggressive than anything. (I am one of the people and don't you forget it, and who do you think you are anyway, you're no better than I am, just you wait till the revolution etc.) At the same time, what is most apparent in the Planster's vision is its complete disregard for people's individuality, those very qualities that distinguish them as human beings: they are not people; they are 'workers', they are 'Surging Millions' (carefully capitalized as if that were their collective name). They eat soya beans in communal canteens and are addressed through microphones which (and who is speaking?) tell them that everything is just great. It is Orwell's nightmare, and Huxley's, distilled into six lines.

As the earlier poem, 'Slough', makes clear, such bile on Betjeman's part does not extend to the inhabitants:

It's not their fault they do not know
The birdsong from the radio . . .

On the contrary, as with the portrait of Elaine, he treats
them with affection and humour.

We should note that these three poems, although
widely spaced in time over a period of some twenty
years, were all written when the need for a massive building programme was obvious, during the slum-clearing
period of the 1930's and in the re-building period after the
Second World War. Betjeman was aware of these needs,
of course; what he was drawing attention to was the need
for care, for feeling for the environment. This is an unex-
ceptionable sentiment in the 1980's (though the more bar-
barous architects and planners still have to be watched)
but the fact that it is so is due in no small measure to John
Betjeman. He was more often scoffed at than admired for
his attitudes – particularly for his championship of much
Victorian architecture – but he was never one to be
swayed by mere fashion.

All of this suggests a determined crusader, a man fighting a brave and lonely battle against philistine forces. This
in its turn, though, seems to be belied by his public image
which was that of a humorous, slightly eccentric, childlike and somewhat simple person.

His jokes at his own expense are often made in the context of an ostensible portrait of another, usually one of
those large, healthy, amazonian girls of whom he was so
fond.

Oh! would I were her racket press'd
With hard excitement to her breast
And swished into the sunlit air
Arm-high above her tousled hair,
And banged against the bounding ball.
'Oh! Plung!' my tauten'd strings would call,
'Oh! Plung! my darling, break my strings.
For you I will do brilliant things.'
And when the match is over, I

71

Would flop beside you, hear you sigh;
And then, with what supreme caress,
You'ld tuck me up into my press.
Fair tigress of the tennis courts,
So short in sleeve and strong in shorts,
Little, alas, to you I mean,
For I am bald and old and green.

'The Olympic Girl'

The sad folly of his longing for the girl is accentuated by
the absurd image of himself as a tennis racket being
powerfully wielded, then tucked up, the absurdity being
heightened still more by the mock-sexuality envisaged:
'press'd/With hard excitement to her breast'; the lover's
ecstasy as he is smashed against a tennis ball; the satisfied
exhaustion after the event, 'I would flop beside you, hear
you sigh . . .'

The folly of human beings was a constant source of
amusement to him. He was still amused, though sharper
in his comments, by a particular form of folly –
pretension.

Objectively, our Common Room
    Is like a small Athenian State –
Except for Lewis: he's all right
    But do you think he's *quite* first rate?

Hampshire mentality is low,
    And that is why they stare at us.
Yes, here's the earthwork – but it's dark;
    We may as well return by bus.

'A Hike on the Downs'

So far we have concerned ourselves mainly with the
'lighter' side of Betjeman's poetry, though we have seen
that 'lightness' can be deceiving. Equally important in his
output, though, are the 'serious' poems, particularly
those that deal with death. 'Webster was much possessed
by death' says T. S. Eliot, rightly, but hardly more so

than was Betjeman. Once again we are struck by an ambiguity: throughout his life Betjeman remained a devout Christian, yet for most of that life (he seems to have been reconciled to it in his last years) he had an inordinate terror of death.

> He would have liked to say good-bye,
>   Shake hands with many friends,
> In Highgate now his finger-bones
>   Stick through his finger-ends.
>
> You, God, who treat him thus and thus,
>   Say 'Save his soul and pray.'
> You ask me to believe You and
>   I only see decay.
>   *'On a Portrait of a Deaf Man'*

Similarly, in 'Late-Flowering Lust', the awful contrast between the ageing couple in their embrace and the ever-nearing inevitability of their death is painfully presented.

> But I've a picture of my own
>   On this reunion night,
> Wherein two skeletons are shewn
>   To hold each other tight;
>
> Dark sockets look on emptiness
>   Which once was loving-eyed,
> The mouth that opens for a kiss
>   Has got no tongue inside.

There are times for him when the consolations of religion are insufficient and he acknowledges these times. Elsewhere his faith is presented with straightforward simplicity.

Betjeman's Christian faith and his lifelong interest in buildings combined to make him an acknowledged expert on English churches. He liked the trappings of religion too: he liked matins and evensong, hymns and psalms.

He also knew the dangers of confusing the trappings with
the real substance of belief:

> Illuminated missals – spires –
> Wide screens and decorated quires –
> All these I loved, and on my knees
> I thanked myself for knowing these
> And watched the morning sunlight pass
> Through richly stained Victorian glass
> And in the colour-shafted air
> I, kneeling, thought the Lord was there.
> Now, lying in the gathering mist
> I know that Lord did not exist;
> Now, lest this 'I' should cease to be,
> Come, real Lord, come quick to me.
> 'Before the Anaesthetic, or A Real Fright'

Even here, in the contemplation of his possible death on
an operating table, Betjeman can afford a little joke at the
expense of man's hopes and fears, for surely the poem's
alternative title is such a joke? Indeed, the final impression that one comes away with from reading Betjeman's poetry is just this: that life on this earth, its hopes
and pretensions, its fears and posturings, even its glories,
ultimately is a sad folly. To counter that we need humour
to reveal the folly, judgment to see the pretensions and
posturings for what they are, and faith to try to cope with
the hopes and fears.

8. Edwin Muir
by
DOUGLAS YOUNG

Edwin Muir was born in Orkney in 1887, where his father was a farmer, and he was brought up there until he was fourteen. He wrote quite brilliantly about this childhood period in his *An Autobiography* which is the best book that one can read as an introduction to the poetry of Muir.

His Orcadian childhood was of great significance for Muir as an adult and as a poet, for it gave to him an image of what life can and ought to be, which he continually brought into contrast with the sad mess that modern civilization has made of things.

The community in which he lived as a child was a traditional one which looked to the past rather than to the new ways of the contemporary world. There was a strong sense of interdependence and co-operation, and a realisation of the relationship not only between men, but between man and the animal world and the whole natural environment around them.

In this harmonious atmosphere, and protected by the security of his family, the child was able to live life to the full. This led Muir to a firm conviction that the child's experience of the world is the most intense and complete experience of reality. In his *An Autobiography* he writes:

> And a child has also a picture of human existence peculiar to himself, which he probably never remembers after he has lost it: the original vision of the world. I think of this picture or vision as that of a state in which the earth, the houses on the earth, and the life of every human being are related to the sky overarching them; as if the sky fitted the earth and the earth the sky. Certain dreams convince me that a child has this vision, in which there is a completer harmony of all things with each other than he will ever know again.

What brings about this removal from Eden is, of course, simply the process of growing up, and the passing of time. In Edwin Muir's imagination, Time itself is seen as a destructive force, destroying not only the innocence of childhood but bringing decay and degeneration throughout nature.

In Muir's own case, the big step came when he was fourteen and the family moved from Orkney to live in Glasgow. There he came into contact with a life-style which could scarcely have been more different from that which he had known in Orkney. What struck him most, was the way that in industrial capitalism all sense of community and co-operation gave way to competitiveness and isolation. In this alien environment his family could not thrive, and within a few years both his parents and his two elder brothers were dead, one of the latter in a particularly painful and grotesque way from a brain tumour. He himself did various dead-end jobs including work in a factory that made charcoal from old animal bones which had fragments of decaying flesh and maggots adhering to them, and gave off the most terrible stench as they were processed.

The nightmare life of Glasgow haunted Muir for the rest of his days, and the contrast between it and the pastoral peace that he had known in his childhood is the most fundamental pattern of his imagination. Time and again in his poetry an image of the Orcadian landscape contrasts with the endless maze of city streets with their jungle-like savagery, to embody the very essence of the good and evil in the world. The fundamental search in Muir's life and in his poetry was to find some way to bring together these intense experiences of good and evil, a way which was not merely a retreat into childhood, but which would combine the peace and security he had known then with a recognition of the very real evil in the modern world.

Muir's Glasgow experience brought him to the very verge of breakdown, both physical and mental, from which he was saved by a most fortuitous marriage to Willa Anderson. She saw that he needed to be taken away from this terrible life, and so they went to London where he began to make a living at writing, initially in journalism, reviewing and criticism. Part of the restorative process involved him in psycho-analysis and this was a very important development, both in terms of his personal well-being and his future poetry. Psycho-analysis taught Muir to attach importance to dreams and to see in them symbolic representations of his own inner conflicts and the conflicts inherent in life itself. Many of his poems are directly based on dreams, and he repeatedly uses the symbols of the unconscious mind to embody in vivid concrete terms, his abstract perception of the nature of existence.

The Muirs spent much of their married life on the continent, where they found it cheaper to live on what they could earn from journalism and the translation of foreign literature, notably the German novels of Franz Kafka. During the 1930's, they lived both in Germany and Italy, and so had had first-hand experience of the growth of fascism which culminated in the Second World War, an experience which confirmed in Muir his conviction of the strong forces of evil at work in modern life.

The outbreak of war brought them back to Scotland.

vays had a strong sense of involvement in Scot-
he could never live there happily. Its history and
present condition seemed to him a prime example of
human potential being destroyed by religious and economic forces. Calvinism and capitalism together had
turned the country into a joyless and inhuman waste-
land, and his poems about Scotland, such as Scotland
1941' and 'Scotland's Winter', contain an anger and bitterness unusual in Muir's work.

After the war they returned to Europe and he worked
for the British Council in Prague, and they were there
during the Communist take-over of Czechoslovakia in
1948. This was again a vivid experience of the power of
evil. A nation which was just picking itself up from the
horrors of war and years of German occupation was suddenly plunged once more, into an atmosphere of op-
pression and terror, and his personal involvement had a
vivid and depressing effect upon Muir's imagination.
In his *An Autobiography* he writes:

> The stories about the Nazis when I first came to
> Prague, and those I heard now about the
> Communists, called up a vast image of impersonal
> power, the fearful shape of our modern humanity.

From Prague the Muirs moved to Rome where the pervasive religious atmosphere helped Muir towards seeing
this problem of evil in the world in more explicitly Christian terms, though he never attached himself to any particular church or religious faith. His last few years were
spent in Britain, at first as warden of Newbattle Abbey,
a residential college for adults near Edinburgh, and then
in retirement near Cambridge, where he died in 1959.

Muir is unusual as a poet in that he started writing
poetry relatively late in life and got better as he got older.
He was well into his thirties when he began, and one
feels that these early poems are part of that process of
'sorting himself out' after the trauma of his Glasgow experience. His first book of poetry was published in 1925

and it attaches much importance to childhood and to the child's vision of the world. There is therefore always the danger of nostalgia, of a plaintive longing for what has been and cannot be recaptured. The contemporary world hardly comes into these early poems.

This theme of childhood remembered is to be found in the very first poem in the book, which remains as the first poem in his *Collected Poems*, simply called 'Childhood'. The images of sunshine, security, timelessness, together with the almost childlike simplicity of the stanza form and the rhymes, capture very well the remembered feeling of peace and well-being that he is trying to recreate. The landscape is clearly Orkney, with a boy sitting on a hillside, on an island looking out over the water to the unknown islands on the horizon and a world which he will one day enter. The blackness of the islands out there seems to contrast with the warmth and security of his present life, bound as he is to the protectiveness of his father's house. This world beyond his childhood ken is mysterious, the colours vague, shrouded in mist, not differentiated or detailed in any way in his mind, but with the limited experience that he has of the world he can see them only as places of still light, tranquility and joy. He lives only for the present and all of time seems for him to be contained in how long it takes for a ship to pass before him. And so he exists in total harmony with the small and immediate world around him, motionless as the rocks which may be sleeping, but which have a life just like his own, with the final security of home, and his mother, and his name being called.

The poem which follows this in the first book, 'Horses', is also an attempt to recapture childhood and the very special way that the child experiences the world. It is based on a real memory of his own life on the farm, and is about the sense of loss of that very acute childish responsiveness, a complex mixture of dread and awe and reverence amounting almost to a sense of magic which he then felt towards these animals. As an adult he sees them only as lumbering creatures moving across a bare

and stony field, and then suddenly he and they are transformed as the childhood vision re-awakens and they become wild and strange creatures of terror and magic. In
detail he remembers the power of their hooves and the
feeling of awe that they inspired as if they were angelic
creatures. Their bodies exude light and some 'mysterious
fire', their eyes a 'cruel apocalyptic light', a revelation of
some supernatural force. All is power and energy and intensity. And then that childish vision fades and he is back
to the bare world of adult consciousness regretting that
he can no longer dwell in that 'dread country crystalline'
where experience was hard and clear-cut and intensely
bright.

This concern for childhood and the ideal which it represents remains with Muir throughout his life, but what
is added in his later poetry is the ability to face up to the
dark realities that his adult experience has taught him,
not in terms of direct comment on the events of his time
but by means of symbolic dramas which embody the essential meanings of recent history. A good example of
this is 'The Combat', a deceptively simple poem which
yet contains a great deal of meaning.

The story seems straight-forward enough, an account
of a fight between two unevenly-matched opponents.
The result appears to be a foregone conclusion but, as
often happens in these circumstances, the favourite does
not achieve the expected easy victory. His feeble opponent simply will not give in, so that there is no real end
to the fight, though in the last few lines there is just the
suggestion that the great one is being betrayed by his
own frustration and fury.

It is when we ask ourselves who the two combatants
are that the difficulty starts. Any attempt to identify them
with real creatures from nature is unhelpful. Each combines bits and pieces from different creatures, like in fact
the strange composites that we do sometimes encounter
in our dreams, and indeed Muir has told us that the
poem is based on an actual dream that he had.

It is set in that vague landscape which we experience

in our dreams, and we must interpret the two combatants as if they were symbols in a dream. One seems to embody all that is powerful and magnificent. Made up of all the most arrogant and regal of animals, there is, too, a ruthlessness and viciousness suggested by the claws and whetted beak. His opponent is the very opposite of this, shabby and weak, apparently without value or advantage, but persevering.

Any attempt to say more specifically what the poem is about depends upon each one of us seeking from our own experience something which corresponds with this kind of conflict. Muir had lived in Glasgow in the years leading up to and during the First World War, and had been greatly distressed by the abject hopelessness of the unemployed. The conflict here could perhaps be a representation of the class war with that poor rejected creature, the victim of the ruthlessness of capitalism. Then again Muir had lived through the rise of Hitler in Germany and seen at first hand the arrogance and viciousness of totalitarianism and the wretched plight of the refugees. The poem was in fact written after his Czechoslovakian experience where he had seen 'the fearful shape of our modern inhumanity'. In his autobiography he talks about a victim of this communist horror – 'and my eyes came back again and again to the worn and patched soles of her boots, a battered image of her own constancy and humble faith. I did not feel that this ancient humanity could ever be destroyed by the new order'.

What – if any – of all this is the poem about? The answer in a sense is that it is about all of it – or none of it. The essence of Muir's symbolic method is that he does not write specifically about this or that incident or experience, but of the essential common feature, the neverending struggle of good and evil that is manifest in all of these specific cases and many more, for it is an inherent characteristic of the life process itself.

Another poem which operates through the same kind of dream symbolism is 'The Grove'. Here the story is of someone labouring up a hill. Getting up through the lower slopes is hard going for they are covered in dense jungle-like undergrowth, but suddenly the climber gets through all this and comes out on to a calm and open hill-top where he can see and comprehend the world around him. The hill-top reminds us of that boy in the early poem, 'Childhood', for it brings the same sense of peace and harmony, but the question now is how that state is to be recaptured, for that jungle-like undergrowth is there and must be gone through. With the brilliant surrealism of dream, Muir depicts this grove as an image of all the terror and horror of civilization. It is a nightmare vision of power and ruthlessness, animal passion and arrogance. The decadence and perversion of it all is summed up in the magnificent line,

> The sweet silk-tunicked eunuchs singing ditties.

This jungle is the world as we have made it and it must be faced up to. The poem begins with the assertion,

> There was no road at all to that high place
> But through the smothering grove

and ends with the same assertion. A sense of inner-calm and harmony cannot be achieved by escaping from the realities of the modern world but only by immersing one-self in them. Paradoxically a commitment to human suffering brings its own state of grace; we can come through the nightmare jungle to see the world set before us in splendour.

A very similar vision of the modern world as a night-mare maze in which we appear to be trapped lies at the heart of another well-known poem, 'The Labyrinth', and it is an awful picture of reality which clearly haunted Muir's imagination. 'Why have we got ourselves into this position?' is the question to which he addresses himself in his poem, 'The Castle'. This poem, too, seems to ema-nate from Muir's experience of the War and from his time in Prague and can be seen as an attempt to explore in his imagination the circumstances that have allowed such terrible situations to arise. The inhabitants of the castle appear to be secure, lying at ease in the summer warmth rather like the boy in 'Childhood'. The enemy is distant and the fortress seems impregnable, but the betrayal comes from within. The sense of security is allowed to become complacency and no thought is given to 'the little wicked wicket gate'. The almost playful nature of the phrase underlines the little importance that is given to this gate, but it, combined with the lure of gold, brings the whole edifice to disaster. Complacency, a lack of vigilance, material self-interest, these the poem seems to say, are what have brought our civilization to ruin.

The two short poems, 'Suburban Dream' and 'The Late Wasp', appear slight pieces, but they show how in fact Muir's poetry as a whole does hang together for they touch upon themes that are treated more intensely in those poems which we have just been looking at. 'Suburban Dream' shares with 'The Grove' and 'The Castle' a contrast of two ways of living. One, which is here associated with women and children, is a life of sunshine, peace and harmony. The other, which has become dominant, is the masculine life dedicated to business, money-making, and mechanised living. 'The Late Wasp' has a pattern not unlike 'The Castle' for a life of security and regular habit is suddenly destroyed with an inevitability that seems in the nature of things.

The poetry of Edwin Muir divides itself roughly into three periods. There is in the early poems a rather nostalgic regret for the peace and harmony of childhood. In the poems of the middle period which we have just been looking at, there comes a much greater recognition of the power of evil, of the continuing battle of good and evil, and at least at times – as in the last poem mentioned, 'The Late Wasp' – a feeling of despair at the inevitable dominance of evil and the betrayal of innocence. In his last poems Muir finally faces up without despair to the problem of evil in the world and comes to terms with it.

This new-found confidence and optimism is evident in the best-known poem in his last volume of poetry, the poem entitled 'The Horses'. The poem certainly confronts the madness of the modern world for it envisages the worst disaster of all, a nucleur holocaust. But this evidence of man's perversity is now seen not as reason for despair but as an opportunity to return to a more sane way of living.

We hear of a seven-days war which has destroyed the world in a way that parallels the seven days of creation in the Book of Genesis. A small group of survivors are left alone in the world, at first afraid of their silent new existence, but gradually getting used to it until they would not listen to their radios, which might speak of the old world that is gone. They have abandoned the tractors which represent the mechanisation of modern civilization, and returned to a more natural use of oxen, gone back to a way of life which their ancient forefathers once lived. This transformation is symbolised by the fact that they are now able to renew contact with that mysterious spirit that permeates the whole living world, and which is embodied in the horses which come back into their lives. These are the wild and magical creatures that we saw in Muir's earlier poem 'Horses', and what has been recaptured is that true bond between man and the world around him, 'that long-lost archaic companionship' which children can still experience, but which civilized men have lost.

To my mind Muir's greatest poem is the title poem of this final volume, 'One Foot in Eden'. Here man is seen as being caught between two worlds, the ideal of which he is capable and the terrible reality that he has achieved. We still have one foot in Eden, a sense of the potential of life, but have made for ourselves a world of 'famished field and blackened tree' where the harvest is one of 'terror and of grief'. But instead of lamenting this terrible waste of our human potential Muir now sees the evil in the world as having a place, and indeed a positive value. Without evil, life would be less rich; there would be no opportunity for grief and charity, for hope and faith, for pity and love. Good and evil are inseparably bound together and the very existence of evil is part of that glory which is human existence.

One foot in Eden still, I stand
And look across the other land.
The world's great day is growing late,
Yet strange these fields that we have planted
So long with crops of love and hate.
Time's handiworks by time are haunted,
And nothing now can separate
The corn and tares compactly grown.
The armorial weed in stillness bound
About the stalk; these are our own.
Evil and good stand thick around
In the fields of charity and sin
Where we shall lead our harvest in.

Yet still from Eden springs the root
As clean as on the starting day.

Time takes the foliage and the fruit
And burns the archetypal leaf
To shapes of terror and of grief
Scattered along the winter way.
But famished field and blackened tree
Bear flowers in Eden never known.
Blossoms of grief and charity
Bloom in these darkened fields alone.
What had Eden ever to say
Of hope and faith and pity and love
Until was buried all its day
And memory found its treasure trove?
Strange blessings never in Paradise
Fall from these beclouded skies.

from *One Foot in Eden* 1956

This is Muir's final comment on the problem of good and evil which has haunted his poetry and his imagination from the start. He is a poet who has been criticised by some for being too much concerned with these rather abstract and philosophical concepts, instead of writing more directly about the great social and political issues that face us today. Maurice Lindsay, for instance, complains that there is 'a feeling of remoteness' about his poetry and that it is 'often merely escapist'. To my mind this is a mistaken criticism. In his vivid symbolic confrontations of the great forces that undermine human behaviour, Muir is able not only to describe the world that we live in but to give us some deep understanding of its meaning.

9. Philip Larkin
by
IAN CURRIE

Philip Larkin was born in Coventry. Rejected as unfit for military service after graduating from Oxford in 1943, he took a post as a librarian in a small town in Shropshire. Subsequently he served as librarian at a number of Universities and was finally Principal Librarian at Hull University.*

Larkin believes that poetry should provide a simple, straightforward pleasure. As he himself put it, parodying Sir Philip Sidney's famous reference to 'a tale which holdeth children from play and old men from the chimney corner', he hopes that his poetry may 'keep the child from its TV set and the old man from his pub'. He is deeply suspicious of poetry which depends for its effects on learned allusions and references to classical mythology; to appreciate such poetry he has said, 'you have to be terribly educated and have to have read everything'. He prefers language which is more readily understandable. While this means that his poetry makes an immediate impact, it does not necessarily mean that his poems themselves are simple, as can be illustrated by an

* Philip Larkin died in December 1985, after this essay was written.

examination of 'Church Going', which is perhaps his best-known poem.

The title 'Church Going' prepares us for something about going to Church. How that situation is treated will emerge from our examination of the poem. Later we will return to consider the implications of the title.

The first thing we might consider is the formal structure of the poem, which consists of seven stanzas of nine lines each. (It is worth while examining the rhyme scheme in detail to reveal how elaborate it is). Given a stanza form as complicated as this, we would expect some complexity of treatment of the theme, with each stanza indicating a new step in the development or a change of thought or image.

The most striking characteristic of the first stanza is the conversational simplicity of the language with a preponderance of monosyllables. The number of run-on lines and the clever variation of the caesura or pause within each line, masks the complexity of the rhyme scheme so that we are hardly aware of it. The speaker is presumably on a cycle run and stops to visit a church passed on his way. The tone is flippant, almost comic. The speaker steps inside the church once he is sure 'there's nothing going on', which at once gives a clue to his own attitude to church-going. The description of the inside of the church is vague and perfunctory. The 'little books' are presumably hymnals and the furnishings of the altar are dismissed almost contemptuously as 'some brass and stuff up at the holy end'. Notice, however, that the silence is 'unignorable' – the word stands out among the other colloquialisms – and the humour of 'brewed God knows how long'. The onomato-poetic effect of the three stressed syllables at the end of the second line, 'letting the door thud shut', is also noteworthy.

In spite of everything, since he has no hat, he removes his cycle-clips as a mark of respect for the place which he has just dismissed so lightly. Already in the first stanza therefore, there are found conflicting attitudes towards the church.

The next stanza completes the description of the experience on which the whole poem is based. The speaker moves around the church examining its undistinguished features, mounts the lectern and mimics the preacher or lay-reader, and characteristically drops an Irish sixpence in the box at the door as he leaves, since the place, in his opinion, was not worth stopping for.

The fact remains, however, that he did stop at this building which is without any aesthetic appeal, a fact which requires some explanation since he is obviously an agnostic, (elsewhere Larkin has described established religion as 'a vast moth-eaten musical brocade/created to pretend we never die'). The subsequent stanzas consist of a series of direct and indirect questions, the speculations of the speaker on this problem, leading up to the answer in the final stanza.

He assumes that churches will, in time, become totally obsolete, with a few cathedrals kept as museum-pieces. The marked use of alliteration in this stanza, 'cathedrals chronically on show', 'parchment, plate and pyx' and 'let the rest rent-free to rain' indicates that the tone is still fairly jocular, although it is more serious than in the previous two stanzas.

The power of religion may linger on in a corrupt form as superstition, but even that will eventually disappear. Note the use of the archaism 'simples' – herbal remedies, which also suggests the naivety of the 'dubious women'. (You might also like to consider the implications of 'when *dis*belief has gone.')

He wonders who will be the very last person to visit the church as a church, some enthusiastic antiquarian or someone nostalgic for the obsolescent rituals. The language with which he dismisses both – 'some ruinbibber, randy for antique/or Christmas addict counting on a whiff' – indicates that both are hooked on the wrong things, the outward shell and the trappings of religion rather than the substance. Preferably it will be someone like himself who gravitates towards it because he is aware that at one time the church had concentrated in itself the most important events in human life – birth, marriage and death – and consequently will always be of interest for all who are concerned about the serious aspect of life.

Notice how the tone of the poem has progressively deepened from the light and cynical at the beginning to the gravity of the final stanza, the language correspondingly shifting from the familiar to the philosophical. The church is a house 'in whose blent air all our compulsions meet/Are recognised and robed as destinies', a place where all the instincts and drives of our human nature are accepted for what they are, the determiners of our fates.

Larkin also has the ability to introduce occasionally into the familar conversational language a deliberate archaism, which is yet perfectly appropriate to the context. 'Simples' we have already noted and 'accoutred' in the second last stanza is another, all the more striking in that it qualifies 'frowsty barn'.

As we follow the firm logical structure of the poem from the initial scheme, through the series of reflective questions, to the final conclusion, we realise that the title embodies a number of meanings: the individual act of the speaker entering the church, the practice of church-going and the disappearance of the church and the decay of traditional religion.

'Mr. Bleaney' is a subtle poem which repays careful study and underlines the fact that a simple surface may conceal unexpected depths. Formally the poem consists of a series of simple four-line stanzas rhyming a b a b, with each one running on into the next to provide continuity of thought.

The situation is simple. The speaker has rented a room formerly occupied by a certain Mr. Bleaney, whose very name has an unprepossessing ring about it. The carefully chosen words reflect the dreariness of the room and its outlook. The room is sparsely furnished and comfortless (even the electric light bulb is only 60-watt); the curtains are frayed and short; there is no room for luggage, physical or intellectual ('books or bags'); the view is confined to a strip of unkempt, rubbish-strewn land. Notice the extensive use of alliteration in lines 3 and 4 of the first stanza.

The bleakness and drabness of his surroundings lead him to reflect on the character of the former tenant, a process which in turn casts light upon his own. From the gossip of the landlady he puts together a mental picture of his predecessor. Mr. Bleaney worked apparently at 'the Bodies'. The setting is possibly the industrial Midlands, 'the Bodies' a car-body assembly plant. The hum-drum pattern of Mr. Bleaney's life is suggested by the selection of detail provided. His tending of the landlady's garden, his watching of the T.V. set he has persuaded her to buy; his football-pool coupon and his conventional holidays. The sort of life-in-death which characterises his existence is hinted at in the opening stanza – 'He stayed the whole time he was at the Bodies till/They moved him'. 'They' are presumably his employers and he was merely trans-ferred to another job, but the unrelated use of 'They' and the word 'Bodies' and 'moved' conjures up an image of undertakers, which the phrase 'one hired box' in the final stanza tends to reinforce.

In the final two stanzas the speaker's anxiety that he may repeat the chilling life-pattern of the previous oc-cupant is underlined by the use of 'frigid wind', 'fusty bed', 'shivered', 'shaking off the dread'. He wonders whether the latter had ever pondered on the apparent failure of his life, since one's environment clearly is a re-flection of one's character and situation.

From the evidence in the poem the answer is – prob-ably not. Mr. Bleaney seems to have been content with his rather solitary, commonplace existence. He appears to be what psychiatrists would call a well-adjusted per-son. It is the sensitive, reflective speaker who is de-pressed by his surroundings and conscious of the implications for his own self-esteem. His only consolation is the discrepancy in their ages; Mr. Bleaney appears to have been coming to the end of his career, while the speaker still has his before him.

Note again how Larkin can vary the tone within the poem from the colloquialisms of 'stub my fags', 'egged her on' and 'plugging at the four aways' to the reflective attitude of the last two stanzas.

The poem 'The Whitsun Weddings' again illustrates Larkin's ability to take a specific experience and invest it with a more general significance and use it as a comment on the human condition. Like 'Church Going', 'The Whitsun Weddings' has an elaborate stanza form of nine iambic pentameter lines rhyming a b a b c d e c d e, i.e. it is like one type of Elizabethan sonnet with the second quatrain omitted. The second line of each stanza, however, is reduced to four syllables and the iambic line is used, as always in Larkin's poetry, with great freedom.

The central event in this instance is a train journey by the poet from the North of England to London (the reference to Lincolnshire and the broad drifting river, almost certainly the Humber, would seem to indicate that Hull is the point of departure) on the Saturday of a Whit weekend holiday.

The first two stanzas strikingly illustrate the poet's ability to evoke a realistic landscape with vivid details, a series of sense-impressions, as the train makes its slow way South in the early summer heat. The windows of the compartments are down, the cushions hot, the cattle are 'short-shadowed' because of the height of the sun, an idea repeated perhaps in the usual juxtaposition of 'tall heat'. The stench of the harbour is replaced by the occasional smell of grass as the train proceeds into the countryside, deadening 'the reek of buttoned carriage cloth', a phrase which combines olfactory and visual images.

Notice too how the details selected suggest impressions from a moving train; crossing a street is reduced to the flash of car windscreens, a hothouse 'flashes uniquely', and the hedges appear to rise and fall as the train passes.

There is some very effective use of alliteration too: 'canals with floatings of industrial froth' and 'Until the next town, new and non-descript/Approached with acres of dismantled cars', the latter example a succinct evocation of one of the characteristic new towns surrounded by the detritus of the post-war affluent society.

Again it is worth noting how the poet varies the rhythm of the verse as in 'The river's level drifting breadth began/Where sky and Lincolnshire and water meet', where the slower movement enacts the quiet flow of the river.

Whitsun is traditionally a favourite time for weddings and gradually the poet becomes aware that at each station parties of wedding-guests are seeing off newly-weds. As the train pulls out, he notices indeterminate groups, the men grinning with sleek, brilliantined hair, the girls in copies of the latest fashions. They are watching the train pull out 'as if out on the end of an event' – the wedding – and 'waving goodbye to something that survived it' – the marriage.

His curiosity aroused, at the next station he pays more attention. He is now able to distinguish the individual members of each party, notes the wedding finery of the girls. He watches carefully the differing reactions of the individuals to the ceremony they have just celebrated – 'each face seemed to define just what it saw departing'. The children are bored, the fathers see it as a great comic triumph, the knowing older women are conscious of both the pleasant and sad aspects of the event – 'like a happy funeral'. The younger girls, somewhat apprehensively, 'gripping their handbags tighter', view the bride as a sacrificial victim.

The train continues its journey southwards with its freight of a dozen newly-married couples. As it nears London signs of urban development appear, fields have become building plots, and the poplars lining the major roads converging on the capital cast long shadows as the sun declines in the West. The couples are self-contained in their happiness – 'none thought of the others they would never meet'. The poet suddenly sees their destination in the shape of a postal map, each district like a field of wheat.

The poet ends on a positive note. Larkin himself has said that, when read aloud, a sustained note should be held until the very end when it should 'lift off the ground'. As the train slows to enter the main-line terminal, the poet is aware of 'a sense of falling, like an arrow – shower/Sent out of sight, somewhere becoming rain'. Rain is a traditional symbol of life-giving energy; hence the married couples in their changed lives descending on the city have the power to revivify it like a shower of rain falling on the fields of wheat.

The previous three poems are examples of Larkin's ability to develop an experience in a logical, rational, unassertive manner towards some reflective conclusion. The remaining poems in *Gallery* vary from the more directly lyrical 'Coming', with its fresh response to the approach of Spring, and the restrained pathos of 'The Explosion', to the bitter, scathing attack on the consequences of progress on England's green and pleasant land, in 'Going, Going'.

10. Ted Hughes
by
IAN CURRIE

Ted Hughes was born in the West Riding of Yorkshire and attended Pembroke College, Cambridge. He began by studying English but switched during the course to the study of anthropology. This was a significant change for mythology has played a major role in his later poetry.

In his early work, however, his subject matter is largely the natural world and man's relationship to it. In particular, he was interested in animals, an interest which he traces back to his earliest years. At the age of three he already had a collection of toy lead animals, and later at threshing time on the farm he would catch the mice from under the sheaves. Although animals fascinated him, there is nothing sentimental in his relationship to them. His natural world is not the world of Peter Rabbit and Benjamin Bunny; it is rather nature as described by Tennyson – 'red in tooth and claw'. As a child he found dead animals as interesting as live ones; his elder brother would bring home magpies, owls, rabbits, weasels and so on. Hughes has commented 'He could not shoot enough for me'.

Hughes is very much aware of the predatory nature of the animal kingdom and believes that man, although marked off from the natural world by self-consciousness, is nevertheless very much part of it and shares many of its

fundamental drives and impulses. It is significant that of
the six poems selected for this anthology, five deal with
animals, three of which are savage predators, the fourth
can be dangerous and untrustworthy and the attributes
of the one domestic animal described are not those generally associated with it in the public consciousness.

Hughes's attitude to animals can perhaps best be illustrated by a poem, 'Thrushes'.

Terrifying are the attent sleek thrushes on the lawn,
More coiled steel than living – a poised
Dark deadly eye, those delicate legs
Triggered to stirrings beyond sense – with a start, a
    bounce, a stab
Overtake the instant and drag out some writhing thing.
No indolent procrastinations and no yawning stares,
No sighs or head scratching. Nothing but bounce and
    stab.
And a ravening second.

Is it their single-mind-sized skulls, or a trained
Body, or genius, or a nestful of brats
Gives their days this bullet and automatic
Purpose? Mozart's brain had it, and the shark's mouth
That hungers down the blood-smell even to a leak of its
    own
Side and devouring of itself: efficiency which
Strikes too streamlined for any doubt to pluck at it
Or obstruction deflect.

With a man it is otherwise. Heroisms on horseback,
Outstripping his desk diary at a broad desk,
Carving at a tiny ivory ornament
For years: his act worships itself – while for him,
Though he bends to be blent in the prayer, how loud
    and above what
Furious spaces of fire do the distracting devil's
Orgy and Hosannah, under what wilderness
Of black silent waters weep.

There is no need to analyse this poem in detail. What Hughes obviously admires in the thrushes (although the inversion in the first line places the word 'terrifying' in the emphatic position at the beginning, it is a terrified fascination) is the hard singleness and strength of their 'bullet and automatic purpose', the streamlined efficiency of their hair-trigger reactions. In contrast to man with his hesitations and vacillations, his tendency to be distracted, the bird seems to have an enviable, instant, instinctive response in the struggle for survival.

Formally the poem 'The Jaguar' is written in a four-line stanza. Although Hughes frequently dispenses with rhyme altogether, here there is a pattern of rhymes and half-rhymes which is worth studying.

The first two verses set the scene, which is obviously in a zoo, and with a few deft, sensuous touches the poem provides a vivid impressionistic description of some of the animals. The bored apes 'adore their fleas in the sun', evokes a picture of the loving care with which they groom one another. The parrots 'shriek as if they were on fire' and are compared to prostitutes trying to entice clients. Notice the preponderance of 'r' and 't' and 's' sounds combined in the first verse, sounds which echo the raucous cries of the parrots, and how the two comparisons emphasise the flashy, gaudy plumage of the birds.

The tiger and lion are paradoxically 'fatigued with indolence'; confinement and lack of exercise have made them tired and lazy. The immobility and the shape of the sleeping snake, like a huge petrified shell, are conveyed by the image 'The boa-constrictor's coil is a fossil'. The balanced alliteration of 'Cage after cage seems empty, or /Stinks of sleepers from the breathing straw' reinforces the impression of the somnolent lethargy of the animals. There is nothing to disturb the observer here, no menace or threat – 'It might be painted on a nursery wall'.

The remaining stanzas describe a contrasting scene. The spectators whose attention has not been held by these animals, cluster round the cage containing the jaguar. The crowd are fascinated by the fierce, angry energy of the savage beast pacing relentlessly round its compound. The concentrated, explosive destructive power of the animal is stressed as the poet describes it 'hurrying enraged/Through prison darkness after the drills of his eyes/On a short fierce fuse'.

In contrast to the other animals, however, it is not boredom that makes it apparently oblivious to its surroundings, 'the eye . . . blind' and 'deaf the ear', but the throbbing, pulsing energy of its being enacted by the reiterated explosive 'b' sounds of 'blind the fire/By the bang of blood in the brain'. 'He spins from the bars', catches the wheeling movement of the jaguar as it changes direction within the narrow confines of its cage, but although, of course, it is objectively enclosed, subjectively it is a free spirit like the saint or mystic in his cell – 'his stride is wildernesses of freedom'. As it paces its cage, the world seems to be turned by the power of its stride. Such fierce energy can never be tamed or dominated by physical constrictions.

The jaguar was seen from the point of view of an observer. However the poem, 'Hawk Roosting' represents the bird's thoughts. Formally it is written in four-line stanzas, unrhymed, the number of syllables in each line varying from eleven to six.

The poem begins with a simple statement, each word a monosyllable – 'I sit on the top of the wood, my eyes closed'. The bird then hastens to add that this is merely a period of rest, 'inaction'; the bird is not dreaming – introducing illusions between itself and the real world – 'no falsifying dream/Between my hooked head and hooked feet', but perhaps rehearsing in its mind's eye the tactics for the next kill. The emphasis is on the hawk's offensive weapons, the hooked head and feet, beak and talons.

In hunting its prey, the hawk makes use of all its natural advantages, the height of the trees, the air and the sun. The air allows him to hover with the sun's glare behind him, which blinds its prey to the threat hanging over it. (This tactic was adopted by the fighter pilots during the war, hence the RAF's warning to its aircrew, 'Beware the Hun in the Sun.') The last line of the second verse, 'and the earth's face upward for my inspection' not only describes the bird's eye view, but stresses the control of the hawk over its territory.

The next verse shows how the hawk is the culmination of the long process of evolution of the animal kingdom, a realm which he now dominates. When he soars and circles, the earth seems to turn beneath him but the poet, by using the verb 'revolve' transitively rather than intransitively, as might be expected, emphasises the bird's control of the situation. 'I revolve it all slowly'; the hawk imposes its will over the earth.

It is lord of all it surveys. 'There is no sophistry in my body'. The hawk's mode of life is without dissimulation or hypocrisy; it is the savage dealing of death, 'tearing off heads', 'the allotment of death'. Its purpose is unswerving, 'direct through the bones of the living' and no justification is required for its conduct; 'The sun is behind me', an ambiguous line which can be taken literally, as we have already seen, and can also be interpreted as a statement of the law of nature, the sun being a symbol of nature with its pitiless law of kill or be killed.

The final stanza again stresses the complete control of the hawk, the poem ending as it began with a firm, assertive statement of monosyllables: 'I am going to keep it like this'.

The feeling of cold calculation created by the poem is produced by the unusually large number of abstract expressions used: 'inaction', 'falsifying', 'rehearse', 'convenience', 'advantage' and so on.

In an interview, the poet said, 'That bird is accused of being a fascist . . . the symbol of some horrible genocidal dictator. Actually what I had in mind was that in this hawk Nature is thinking. Simply Nature'. This may well be so but it is difficult to resist the feeling that the poet admires the hawk's intensity of purpose. It may be instructive to compare the treatment of the same bird by Gerard Manley Hopkins in 'The Windhover'. Here the attribute of the bird which the poet admires is the beauty of its flight, its mastery of the air, although he is quite conscious of the menace behind it.

The poem 'The Pike' takes as its subject matter a fish which has the reputation of being one of the most ravenous of its kind. It falls naturally into three parts; the first four verses give a sketch of the pike, the next three supply two specific examples of its rapacity, and the last four describe its effect on the poet.

The first section emphasises the combination of beauty and ferocity: the green 'tigers' the gold, they are 'killers from the egg', their grin is 'malevolent'. Notice the extensive use of alliteration throughout the poem and particularly here where the preponderance of 'p' and 'g' sounds seem to underline the grinning indignity of the pike. Giants among the other pond life, they are 'silhouettes of submarine delicacy and horror'.

The coinage 'logged' suggests the heavy stillness of the pike lurking on the decaying leaves at the foot of the pond and 'hung' the suspended animation in its cave of weeds. Noticeable again is the variety of reference to colour in these opening verses: 'green', 'gold', 'emerald', 'black', 'amber'.

The fourth verse concentrates on the shark-like jaws of the pike, evolved to perfection for the essentially predatory nature of its existence – 'a life subdued to its instrument'.

The next three stanzas give instances of the savage cannibalism of the pike, 'jungled in weed'. By means of the inversion in the first line of verse five, 'Three we kept behind glass', the poet highlights the swift transition from three to one by the end of the verse, a change reflected also in the more staccato rhythm of the lines. Like the shark in 'Thrushes' whose mouth 'hungers down on the blood-smell even to a leak of its own/Side and devouring of itself', the pike's killer instinct can lead to self-destruction; the ferocity of the attack is summed up in the balanced alliteration of 'jammed past its gills down the other's gullet'. The pitiless determination of the fish is echoed in the 'vice' and the 'iron in the eye'.

In the final verses the poet himself intrudes, with his memories of a particular pond he fished, presumably as a boy, a pond as old as England itself – 'as deep as England' – where the flora and fauna, the lilies and the tench, had survived all human artefacts. Within its depths huge pike lurked which aroused so much apprehension in him that after dark he was afraid to cast his line but stiff with fear, he did so.

The most conspicuous linguistic feature of these last verses is the use of repetition: 'immense', 'cast', 'move' and 'darkness' are all repeated. It is clear that this device is used to indicate that the poem is operating here on two levels – the natural level of the outside world, the pond and the pike, the owls and the trees, and a second, inner, unconscious level. As the fearsome pike might rise from the still depths of the dark lake, so from the dark depths of his unconscious mind something stirs and rises. The hooting of the owls in the trees reflected in the water is almost eliminated from his consciousness by the dream which has been conjured up by 'the darkness beneath night's darkness', a primitive, unconscious impulse.

A syntactical feature of the poem is the frequent omission of the tenses of the verb 'to be'. Repeatedly, the sentences lack a verbal predicate: 'Pike, three inches long' . . .; 'A hundred feet long in their world'; 'In ponds . . . gloom of their stillness'; 'the same iron in his eye'; and so on. This contributes to the impression of compactness and compression in the poem.

The poem 'The Bull Moses' is a complex poem which combines accurate observation and imaginative reflection. The poem moves continually between a simple external reality, the physical description of the bull, to a consideration of the mystery of its seeming power, and to the mind of the observer.

The first section describes the small boy being lifted up to be able to look over the half-door of the byre into the bull's stall. Note the neat coinage 'ledged' and the paradoxical 'Blaze of darkness' which both emphasises the intensity of the blackness and points to what it causes: 'a sudden shut-eyed look/Backward into the head', that is a sudden insight into the mind. From the external world of the bull we have entered the inner consciousness of the observer. Hughes has said that 'the bull presents what the observer sees when he looks into his own head'. The gnomic statement 'Blackness is depth/Beyond star' seems to mean that the depths of the mind are unfathomable.

Once again we return to the sensuous detail of the physical reality of the bull, its warmth and smell, the massive solidity of the brow 'like masonry' and the strength of the neck, 'deep-keeled' like the underside of a ship, but again this immediately summons up something indeterminate and indistinct from the depth of the unconscious mind to the brink of the conscious mind.

Again we return to the world of the bull, a world which seems to be totally divorced from that of the farmer and the boy; 'the square of sky' of the byre door which represents the world means nothing to him.

The bull seems to be completely docile, entirely under the control of the farmer as he is led each evening to the duck-pond to drink. He seems devoid of interest in his past and his progenitors, content to inhabit his restricted world, completely dominated by external reality symbolised by the brass ring through his nostrils. He appears to be oblivious to his environment, the sights and sounds of which stir no response in 'the locked black of his powers'. He strolls quietly back to his byre but the observer is aware that these deep black forces *are* there and the bolt on the door ensures that they are kept under restraint.

The bull is subject to the control of the farmer, but yet so totally self-contained and removed from the farmer's world that its existence can hardly be called a state of subjection since, like the jaguar's cage, the farmer's world is an irrelevance. In the same way, perhaps, the conscious mind appears to be able to dominate the dark forces of the unconscious, but occasionally we catch glimpses of the hidden power in the depths.

Of the remaining two poems in the anthology 'Esther's Tomcat' and 'Dick Straightup', only this need now be said; the thing that Hughes admires in both the cat and the man is their ability to survive, their fierce clinging on to life in all circumstances. It may also be significant that in his account of the cat and the Knight, the poet suppresses the fact that in the original legend the cat died too.

11. Norman MacCaig
by
JOHN BLACKBURN

An invisible drone boomed by
With a beetle in it; the neighbour's yearning bull
Bugled across five fields. And an evening full
Of other evenings quietly began to die.

Since the publication in 1955 of the collection of poems
called *Riding Lights*, Norman MacCaig has been regarded
as an accomplished poet. Critics have praised his powers
of perception, both of the world outside himself and of the
inner goings-on in his own mind. They have praised, too,
his inventiveness with metaphor, his precision, his skill in
handling the rhythms of speech, the effects to be had from
rhyme in all its various forms. His talent for writing neat,
well-structured poems which often end with clever punch
lines has also brought applause.

Yet critics have had harsh things to say about some
aspects of his work. Hugh MacDiarmid, for instance, although careful to draw attention to the admirable features
of his friend's poetry, was wont to declare that MacCaig
could never be a poet of any major significance because
he had not attached himself to any political or cultural
movement or world-view which would enable his poetry
to become powerful, and relevant to society in the twentieth century. Other critics have been perturbed by the

poet's witty, at times almost too clever, play with words and ideas. This, they have said, has led him into writing too much flippant poetry which at times only mystifies the reader. R. W. Scott, writing in *Lines Review* in 1969, had this to say:

> 'He is playful, he pulls off his conjurer's tricks not only with words and images but also with ideas. He is an intellectual con-man and one may be forgiven for asking if there is in fact anything at the end of the garden path . . .. The reader may well feel cheated when a poet sets off on an interesting path and suddenly sidesteps and vanishes with a whimsical goodbye.'

Obviously we have in MacCaig one whose poetry arouses both admiration and aggravation. Let's see what we can make of it, starting with 'Summer Farm', one of the poems from *Riding Lights*.

Straws like tame lightnings lie about the grass
And hang zigzag on hedges. Green as glass
The water in the horse-trough shines.
Nine ducks go wobbling by in two straight lines.

A hen stares at nothing with one eye,
Then picks it up. Out of an empty sky
A swallow falls and, flickering through
The barn dives up again into the dizzy blue.

I lie, not thinking, in the cool, soft grass,
Afraid of where a thought might take me – as
This grasshopper with plated face
Unfolds his legs and finds himself in space.

Self under self, a pile of selves I stand
Threaded on time, and with metaphysic hand
Lift the farm like a lid and see
Farm within farm, and in the centre, me.

The first thing likely to strike the reader of this poem is the imagery. The first three verses are built up almost entirely of images. And they are arrestingly good ones. 'Straws like tame lightnings', water which is 'green as glass', 'ducks wobbling by' and that hen which looks 'at nothing with one eye, then picks it up'. Someone once said that a hen has only two emotions: curiosity and sheer panic. Likewise, it has two outstanding physical characteristics. Every time it takes a step its head jerks forward – step jerk, step jerk, step jerk – ridiculous. Then, to look well at things, since its eyes are set in the side of its head, it cocks its head sideways. What it looks at is frequently too small for us to see from where we observe the hen and so

A hen stares at nothing with one eye,
Then picks it up.

With a dart and a jerk. To human observers there is something daft about hens. And so, on to the swallow and to the poet lying in the cool soft grass, unwilling to start his mind thinking, while a grasshopper nearby unfolds his legs and gets a surprise.

Now it *seems* that what we have here in this bright carnival of images is MacCaig wittily, precisely, describing the world around him as he lies there in the grass. But consider. Is the grasshopper really surprised that it should have taken off so quickly into the air? Of course it isn't. Grasshoppers just do that sort of thing without thinking about it. And what about the hen? Does it really pick up nothing? And do the ducks have any notion that waddling is close to wobbling? And do straws ever have an ambition to be lightnings? No. The truth is that MacCaig in this poem is not describing these hens and ducks and straws as one would 'normally' observe them, even with an attentive eye, in the process of everyday living. What he is doing is inventing, creating, a little world of comical things – frustrated straws, ridiculous hens, astonished grasshoppers and ducks managing to walk in two straight lines but wobbling around all the same. Whatever the world 'out there' really is (and that is a problem which has exercised philosophers for centuries) MacCaig is not concerned to describe it as we think we normally see it. He is, rather, presenting us with a make-believe world. MacCaig's world of the comic and the absurd in which he himself often plays a major, and unflattering part.

By way of emphasising the matter of make-believe, consider, before tackling that last, rather baffling, verse of 'Summer Farm', another poem in which can be seen the same distinctively MacCaigish blend of precise observation and humanising of creatures which characterises the first three verses of 'Summer Farm'.

Wild Oats

Every day I see from my window
pigeons, up on a roof ledge – the males
are wobbling gyroscopes of lust.

Last week a stranger joined them, a snowwhite
pouting fantail,
Mae West in the Women's Guild.
What becks, what croo-croos, what
demented pirouetting, what a lack
of moustaches to stroke.

The females – no need to be one of them
to know
exactly what they were thinking – pretended
she wasn't there
and went dowdily on with whatever
pigeons do when they're knitting.

The same whimsical, gently mocking tone, the same imposing on the world of creatures behaviour which belongs to people, the same skill in handling the flow of the language, the same comic wit. And just the same as in 'Summer Farm' there is an ambiguous quality in the mocking. It is directed at the birds, yet, was the hen really seeing nothing or was it the observer who was ridiculous because his eyesight wasn't good enough to see what the hen saw? And here, the pigeons are apparently the object of the fun, but what about people? Really, all that's being said about the pigeons blows back into the world of men. That's just what we are like too. Poems like this have the merit of being entertaining and easy to grasp at a first reading or hearing, but when they are scrutinised it turns out that there is something quite clever and quite complex going on in them.

Now, what about that last verse in 'Summer Farm', the one which is so different from the rest of the poem? At first sight it looks like the kind of writing to which R. W. Scott took objection in his review. It mystifies. Moreover, when we look more closely at it, we find that it doesn't hold together all that well. A pile of selves is mentioned, yet that pile is threaded as if on a line with all the selves standing upright. That's not a pile. Then what is a metaphysic hand? And in all the farms within farms, like tins within tins presumably, what is the me that is in the centre? Is it one of the selves, or some essential quality in all the selves, something that endures through all the time and change around it? Things are not clear; one begins to feel uneasy about possible garden paths.

Yet pause. Despite the obscure and contrary elements in these lines, this verse is making an important comment on what has gone before in the poem. MacCaig, it seems, although 'Afraid of where a thought might take me' has had a thought here, two thoughts indeed, which he has over and over again in his poetry.

For a start, he appears to be himself aware that what has been going on in the first three verses of the poem has not been a description of the everyday 'world of all of us' but rather the creation of a particular, largely comic, world in the mind of the particular MacCaig who lay in the grass on that particular day. He realises that what might be taken for real in the world he describes around him is in fact invented and put there by himself, by the me in the centre of the farm, in the blue of that summer day. Then he also realises that there is a problem about this me: it changes. As he looks back through time, he notices that not one MacCaig is to be seen, but many. We all change moment by moment, day by day, mood by mood. MacCaig is, in short, touching here on the question (one might almost say the problem) of the self and its relation to the world around it.

These matters of identity and relationship form, I think, the central preoccupation in his poetry, the heartlands of MacCaig as we see him through his writing considering who he is, how he changes, how he sees, or invents, the world around him, how he affects other people by being what he is and how other people affect him, where he stands in relation to the creatures of land, sea and air – frogs, goats, basking sharks, flying beetles, horses, hares – and considering, too, what part words play in asking and answering such questions.

Concern about *words* is, in fact, another of the major preoccupations to be found in his poetry. It is indeed bound in with, intermingled with, the other concerns about self and relationships and the ways in which we know, or do not know, about them. MacCaig is very conscious of the fact that words can mislead us in all manner of ways. He distrusts them. They can lead us, he sees, to believe in the existence of 'things' which are not real at all: they can give us false notions about what is around us, inside our heads, under our noses. They can even persuade us to accept whole systems of erroneous beliefs. They can virtually take over our thinking for us without us being aware of what is happening.

MacCaig is, of course, perfectly well aware that he himself can play tricks with language, as in the first part of 'Summer Farm' or in 'Wild Oats'. He is expert at producing and playing with words, images, metaphors and questions. But, the real dangers inherent in language seem never to be far from his mind. In this respect, the little poem 'A Man in My Position' seems to me to be a key poem in his work.

Imagine him in a tearoom, or a bar, or somewhere else of that nature, talking to a girl. He warns her that she should not believe all that he says, because he may be saying only the sort of things which a man in his position, at a teatable or on a bar stool, would say to a pretty girl, even though he might not really mean them. 'Hear my words carefully' he warns, for 'some are spoken/not by me, but/by a man in my position.' He is uncomfortable at the thought that he may be deceiving her, touching her the wrong way with his words. He hates indeed 'this appalling stranger', the shadowy, actor-like being whom he feels accompanying him, looking out through his eyes, using his mouth to say things, taking over his real self from him. So, at the end, he warns the girl again that she should be wary of what he says until the time comes when his love for her will be strong enough to ensure that anything he says will be genuine, heartfelt, and not just the words of a man, any man more or less, chatting up a girl.

Here then, we have the concern about the self, who he is, – himself or only a bundle of clichés and pretended feelings wrapped up in his form, a talking zombie. And we have, too, the concern about words and their power to deceive. It is a small poem, but it belongs, I think, right in the heart of MacCaig's thinking, and his poetry.

We've seen MacCaig, then, indulging in comic make-believe, and we've seen him wondering about himself and about his connections with the life going on round about him, and we've seen him being edgy about words and their capacity to deceive. Now, not surprisingly, one thing he seems very clear about and that is his dislike of people who, in one way or another, cheat by means of words. (He is none too fond, either, of people who allow themselves to be cheated by words.) One such cheat is to be found in 'Smuggler'.

Watch him when he opens
His bulging words – justice,
Fraternity, freedom, internationalism, peace,

Peace, peace. Make it your custom
To pay no heed
To his frank look, his visas, his stamps
And signatures. Make it
Your duty to spread out their contents
In a clear light.

Nobody with such luggage
Has nothing to declare.

Here we have an angry poem. The subject of the anger
is familiar enough, the speaker, probably a public
speaker, – politician, union leader, or the like – who
manipulates people with his words. The whole piece is
couched in the metaphor of the customs check: the words
have to be opened. They are bulging with false, misleading meaning and we are urged to make it our custom to
ignore all the gestures and shows of authority and to
spread out the meanings of the words in such a way that
they can be truly seen for what they are. There's nobody
with words like these who hasn't got something hidden
that he ought to come clean about.

MacCaig, like Crichton Smith, is a puritan for the truth.
He keeps a sharp eye open for it himself and he is hard
on both fools and hypocrites, those who use words care-
lessly or deceitfully. Many readers and listeners, I think,
underestimate the importance of this element in his
work. It seems that the light, casual, self-focused nature
of much of his poetry tends to draw attention away from
the sharper, more sombre undertones in it, so that he is
seen as a lightweight, dilettante poet, an entertainer,
rather than a writer to be taken seriously. This image of
him, and of his poetry, is hardly discouraged by his own
habit of being dismissive about his poems, saying that
they only take one or two fags to write and by his willingness to give very entertaining public readings of his
poetry. But it's well to remember that poets often prefer
not to discuss their poems in any detail and tend to ward
people off from doing so by being facetious or openly and

sometimes mysteriously, non-committal about them. It is as well to remember, too, that most good comics, funny men, are said to be sad and unsure at heart. MacCaig *is* an entertainer, both on the page and in the lecture hall; but he is also a writer possessed of unusually keen insight and intelligence, and of feeling, too, for things that suffer, and for things that just play in the sun, like his frogs at the back of Ben Dorain. The image then, of the whimsical, rather detached entertainer does not adequately express the character of the man or of his poetry.

MacCaig is sometimes criticised as being a limited poet unable to produce major works because he has not committed himself to causes, beliefs and movements which would make it possible for his poetry to be carried forward into greater themes than those provided by his concern with himself and his immediate environment. This criticism has been levelled at MacCaig by people of widely differing views of the world. Marxists have complained, as MacDiarmid did, of his lack of political attachment while Christians have complained of his lack of religion!

There is, I think, a certain rough, and limited, justice in this kind of criticism. MacCaig is not a writer of long, inspiring and optimistic poems. But it seems to me that the reason for MacCaig being a man of short poems and no ideological commitments is one which has to be respected. It should not be difficult by this stage in our consideration of his poetry to see what it is likely to be. He is too well aware of the tricks of language and the harm they can cause, too suspicious, that is, of slogans, generalisations, calls to action and all the other means by which ideologies are created and made to survive to be able to ally himself comfortably with any of them. He would not, I imagine, deny the importance in society of political action, but that doesn't happen to be his particular scene. He is much more at home in the role of the Fool, the wit who calls attention to the nonsense which is being spoken or the damage which is being done in the name of this, that or the other cause. He is the poet who keeps an eye open for smugglers.

So, MacCaig's talent is for the short poem, the particular moment, the penetrating comment. Let's consider now some of the poems he has written in his own style.

'Visiting Hour' is one such. It's one of those poems which seems to come out of a moment when the writer was hurt and disturbed. The hurt, however, is not immediately obvious. The poem begins with MacCaig walking along the corridors of the hospital. They are full of the smell of hospital, that awesome blend of wax polish and disinfectant, and they are green and yellow.

> Green and yella, green and yella,
> Oh help me quick, I'm gonna be sick. . .

There's an overwhelming student song to this effect and I've no doubt that the colours green and yellow make more suitable companions for the hospital smell than would, say, blue and pink. Then there are those nostrils. MacCaig* has a distinguished face with a fairly prominent and also distinguished nose and it's easy to imagine it being bobbed along the corridors by his long, hill-walking, legs. So, in these opening lines we meet the by-now-familiar facetious, self-deprecating tone. Following this, a body is trundled into a lift and vanishes upward, heavenward perhaps.

MacCaig is doing here what he often does in poems like this which involve upset: he is playing the fool, being facetious, unwilling it seems to commit himself to the hurtful part of the poem. Indeed in this poem he explicitly acknowledges this.

* There is, of course, no evidence from the actual text of the poem that it is MacCaig we have to picture here. I think, however, that we can allow ourselves to assume that and so avoid the over-refinement of supposing that he might be writing about someone else or that the poem can only have been written by that strange creature the phantom poet, the Presiding Genius of Pract. Crit. Best I think, at least here, to stay in the world of flesh and blood and imagine, as well as we can, MacCaig. What happens in hospitals, and in this poem, is all too real to be willfully muted by refinements of critical approach.

I will not feel, I will not
feel, until
I have to.

Then the feeling begins as he sees the nurses walking 'here and up and down and there'. He is moved by the bearing of these slim-waisted girls among so much pain and so much sadness.

Ward 7. We come upon the ward in the poem just as we do come upon wards. There it is, suddenly, in front of us, the one we are looking for. And in it 'she' is, in a condition which jolts us at first sight . . . the white cave, the withered hand, the terrible sense of weakness, the wasted arm. These ghost-like images are given further force by their sharing of the letter w, which pulls them together into a sort of singular impact – white, withered, wasted. Set among these images is the fang which is fixed. There is something vicious about the word fang with its almost expletive f sound, reinforced by the same f in fixed. But this fang, the needle of a drip, is 'not guzzling but giving.' I confess I'm a little troubled by the word guzzling here. Its associations for me are with circumstances which are more carefree than what we have here. But then perhaps 'guzzling' is a last flicker of the tone which characterises the start of the poem. At any rate, the rest of the poem flows on in a way which is altogether convincing.

As he sits there beside her, physical distance vanishes from his awareness and he feels very close to her, except that he cannot feel the pain that she does. She manages a little smile as he rises to go, feeling clumsy and dizzy, enveloped in the 'waves' of the time-to-go-bell. As he goes, she sees him grow, not smaller, which would be the normal thing to see, but fainter. She loses, that is, whatever sight of him she has had as soon as he begins to move away from her bedside. All that are left then of the visit are the books which will never be read and the fruits which have been brought in vain.

114

The poem began in the corridors, with MacCaig and his uneasy joke-making; it ends in the ward with the woman left in her world of pain and weakness and whiteness. The joker has gone. There is only a faint smile to remember from across the distance of pain.

In 'Hotel Room, 12th Floor' MacCaig keeps himself in the main focus all the time as the life of New York goes on around him. The poem begins in the same, mildly facetious, way as did 'Visiting Hour'. The helicopter which skirts the Empire State Building is like a damaged insect. We have here the sense, again, of frustrated ambition: the helicopter is not quite the perfect, efficient and symmetrical machine that it might be. Then the Empire State Building is like a jumbo-size dentist's drill. The implication is that it is too big and the word 'jumbo', with its associations with childhood fantasies, adds to the sense of the ridiculous. And, of course, 'Pan Am' has ironic undertones. Pan Am, the company that covers all America, the Pan American. The American obsession with bigness is in MacCaig's sights here.

But these opening lines have more in them than half-comic deprecation of American pretentiousness: there is a sense, too, of threat in the likening of the helicopter to an insect, a damaged insect, and in the dentist's drill. Ominous undertones. And then the comic element disappears. Midnight has come in from foreign, strange and threatening, places in the East, undeterred by the flashing lights being spattered against it, like flashing shots, in the New York sky. The image of shooting is then carried forward and developed as he thinks of the streets and alleyways of the city as if they were the canyons and gulches of the Wild West, and the sirens of the police cars and ambulances as if they were the warhoops of that notoriously unruly region. These things he imagines as he lies between a radio and a television set which, on or off, may be associated with the same locations, the same places of violence and noise. In the second section of the poem, there is created an all-pervading sense of noise, of violence. So we come to the conclusion, the 'wrap-up' lines at the end. The frontier, the place of threat and strife, is never far from us and nothing we can do can keep out the darkness, the horror with which it surrounds us. This is the conclusion our travelling poet drew that particular night as he lay uneasy in New York.

'Brooklyn Cop', another of the 'American' poems, is a fairly straightforward comment on the life of a cop in that dangerous place. The ending of the poem, however, is not simple.

And who would be who have to be
his victims?

That is not simple. It twists the whole poem back on itself and the sense of violence once again becomes all-pervasive.

'Assisi', another of these popular, disturbed, poems, begins with a startling picture of the dwarf 'with his hands on backwards' and his 'tiny twisted legs'. Yet even in this there are still traces of the comic tone. There is a grim, grotesque hint of humour in the backwards hands and the sawdust legs. And there is irony too in the reference to the 'advantage' the dwarf had in still being alive – 'How much does he have to live for?' one would think at a first sight of him. Further irony, I think, in the 'how clever it was of Giotto': that 'how clever it was' is an expression which is frequently used ironically, and after all, painting frescoes to tell stories was a common enough practice in Giotto's time: it was not remarkably clever to think of doing so.

After this grim humour, alongside this vein of irony, run the main lines of the poem. First, there is the contrast between the magnificence of the churches and the ruined temple outside – the dwarf. (The human body is referred to in Christian teaching as the temple of God.) Besides this, there is the dominant theme in the poem, the concern, the indignation, that the tourists should follow the guide like a bunch of hens, eager for the grain of his words while indifferent to the dwarf at the door. Are the guide's words the true grain, that which really merits attention? Is the grain of the Word itself of much use if this is what it produces, clucking tourists? The poem concludes with further shocking details of the dwarf's appearance, he 'whose eyes wept pus' and then with a sudden shift to sweetness, as the voice of the dwarf is likened to that of a child speaking to her mother or a bird speaking to Saint Francis, the saint who cared for the poor and for birds. So the dwarf, is linked through what is beautiful in him, his voice, to the gentleness of the child and the saint and the singing birds, while the clucking tourists and the three tiers of churches disappear from our view.

Although the poems 'Assisi,' 'Hotel Room 12th Floor' and 'Visiting Hour' are among the best known of MacCaig's prolific output, they are not wholly typical of what he writes in that they are more disturbed, more openly expressive of upset feelings than most of his poems are. Usually, as we have seen, whatever feeling is in a poem by MacCaig, it is enveloped within a casual, witty and slightly detached tone so that it is softened and muted. Besides, many of his poems are, by any reckoning, lighthearted ones. Even many of the poems in which the search for self and certainty can be seen are still gay and light. MacCaig has, indeed, been fond of declaring that he is a happy man and, while this essay has been concerned to probe into his poetry to see what makes it tick, it should be noted that along with the more serious poems go many in lighter vein. In *Gallery*, 'Sleeping Compartment' and 'Gone Are the Days' are two such. In both of these he is again, it can be noticed, the subject of his own observations. And I suspect that 'Sparrow', too, is about himself: there are distinct similarities between that bird and its creator.

Recently, however, there has appeared a darker, more openly personal tone in the poetry. In this there are two, fairly distinct, lines of thought. First, we find a certain preoccupation with his own inner darknesses, his own feelings of deficiency and guilt. So we see, in 'Private'

mention of white bandages which it is best to leave on
to hide what is beneath them, and in 'Go Away, Ariel'
he talks, sympathetically with Caliban saying, in the last
lines,

Phone a bat, Ariel. Leave us
to have a good cry – to stare at each other
with recognition and loathing.

Strong words. In an earlier and delightful little poem,
'Toad,' he introduces this introspective darkness more
gently as he contrasts it with the light which a toad has
brought him.

A jewel in your head? Toad,
you've put one in mine,
a tiny radiance in a dark place.

The other darkness which has come into the poetry of
late is that of loneliness, the pervasive loneliness brought
about by the death of old friends and the awareness of
one's own failing energies. Several times he has been
heard to say, 'Don't get old: your friends all die and it's
terrible.' And in *The Listener* not long ago, there was to
be found a short poem which itself lay like a little grave-
stone on the page.

Every day

What's that cart that nobody sees
grinding along the shore road?

Whose is the horse that pulls it, the white horse
that bares its yellow teeth to the wind?

They turn, unnoticed by anyone,
into the field of slanted stones.

My friends meet me. They lift me from the cart and,
the greetings over, we go smiling underground.

That, I think, is a moving poem. It's the kind of poem that should be left as a last word somewhere. But not here. Better here to let MacCaig sign off with one, not about dying, but about life and love, another girl and tea-table poem. The last lines are about giving a cigarette, but there's something in them about MacCaig and his poetry too.

Incident

I look across the table and think
(fiery with love)
Ask me, go on, ask me
to do something impossible,
something freakishly useless,
something unimaginable and inimitable

like making a finger break into blossom
or walking for half an hour in twenty minutes
or remembering tomorrow.

I will you to ask it.
But all you say is
Will you give me a cigarette?
And I smile and,
returning to the marvellous world
of possibility,
I give you one
with a hand that trembles
with a human trembling.

12. George Mackay Brown
by
ALAN MACGILLIVRAY

When you look at the poems by George Mackay Brown printed in *Gallery* as a group, one or two clear impressions leap out at you immediately. The first is that they all come out of an identifiable place with its own distinct characteristics – the Orkney Islands, an area where fishing and farming are very important and where the sea is a constant presence, bringing both a livelihood and the possibility of sudden death to those who sail upon it. The second impression is that the poems are full of characters and incidents and vivid pictures rather than being poems of ideas and comment. There is a considerable degree of truth in both of these impressions. George Mackay Brown was brought up in the small town of Stromness on the Mainland island of Orkney and has lived there for most of his life. He has undoubtedly found in the life and traditions of the islands, a rich source of imaginative fuel for his writing in poetry and prose.

It has been particularly the past of Orkney that has attracted him in his most creative writing. The Orkney that is explored in his poetry is nearly always some distance away from the modern world. Here is a poem which will help you to enter George Mackay Brown's Orkney, showing you the typical place and the typical people of his poetic world.

Hamnavoe

My father passed with his penny letters
Through closes opening and shutting like legends
    When barbarous with gulls
    Hamnavoe's morning broke

On the salt and tar steps. Herring boats,
Puffing red sails, the tillers
    Of cold horizons, leaned
    Down the gull-gaunt tide

And threw dark nets on sudden silver harvests.
A stallion at the sweet fountain
    Dredged water, and touched
    Fire from steel-kissed cobbles.

Hard on noon four bearded merchants
Past the pipe-spitting pier-head strolled,
    Holy with greed, chanting
    Their slow grave jargon.

A tinker keened like a tartan gull
At cuithe-hung doors. A crofter lass
    Trudged through the lavish dung
    In a dream of cornstalks and milk.

In 'The Arctic Whaler' three blue elbows fell,
Regular as waves, from beards spumy with porter,
    Till the amber day ebbed out
    To its black dregs.

The boats drove furrows homeward, like ploughmen
In blizzards of gulls. Gaelic fisher girls
    Flashed knife and dirge
    Over drifts of herring,

And boys with penny wands lured gleams
From the tangled veins of the flood. Houses went blind

Up one steep close, for a
Grief by the shrouded nets.

The kirk, in a gale of psalms, went heaving through
A tumult of roofs freighted for heaven. And lovers
        Unblessed by steeples, lay under
        The buttered bannock of the moon.

He quenched his lantern, leaving the last door.
Because of his gay poverty that kept
        My seapink innocence
        From the worm and black wind;

And because, under equality's sun,
All things wear now to a common soiling,
        In the fire of images
        Gladly I put my hand
        To save that day for him.

If you know Dylan Thomas's play, 'Under Milk Wood',
you will see some similarities – the postman going his
rounds, the gallery of characters from many different oc-
cupations, the progress of the day in the small town from
morning to night. Yet George Mackay Brown's purposes
are very different. Hamnavoe is of course Stromness
where he grew up and there are glimpses of real people
and things that were around him in his boyhood between
the two world wars: the old-style fishing boats with their
sails; the horses from the farms; the Highland fishworkers
gutting and salting the herring catch; the postman (his
father) doing his morning delivery and then the main
delivery in the evening after the 'St Ola' arrived from
Scrabster, using a lantern in winter to read the addresses
on the letters. Yet there is a selection of details to give a
timeless quality to the poem; this is a general time-past
that is apparently untouched by the age of mechanisation. This Hamnavoe exists in an ideal vision of 'seapink
innocence', like himself as a boy, preserved from 'the
worm and black wind' of Progress. George Mackay

Brown has described the purpose of the artist at work in a way that justifies this selection of images from reality to work into a harmonious ideal. 'What the artist tries to create at the centre of his life and time is a place of order, a place of remembrance, a place of vision, to which he returns again and again in times of difficulty and confusion, in order to have things made simple and meaningful once more. It is the workshop of the imagination that fills the world with beautiful shapes.' George Mackay Brown's work as a poet is inspired with this impulse to create an orderly, meaningful and therefore beautiful shape out of his memories and experiences of Orkney, his reading (especially of the Icelandic sagas) and his Catholic faith (gradually developed over many years until his final acceptance in 1961).

Let us look back again at the poem 'Hamnavoe'. We should now be able to see more clearly what is happening in this celebration both of his father's life and of his beloved Orkney. Out of 'the fire of images'the poet plucks the elements for the ideal day that is shaped artificially to sparkle with colour and symbol in contrast to the drab worn-down commonplace reality. The figure of the postman is seen at the start of the day in this small town rich in tradition. The focus of the dawn is the harbour with its raucous gulls and the fishing fleet heading out to reap the cold fields of the sea. Thereafter the day passes in a procession of images – the horse at the trough, the merchants of the town discussing their business and their profits like an act of worship, the tinker begging for scraps of charity at the doors hung with dried fish, the girl from the farm, the afternoon drinkers in the pub, the returning boats full with their catches ready for the herring gutters who sing at their work, the boys fishing with their cheap rods as the tide comes in, death and worship and lovemaking as the night falls and the postman completes his evening delivery.

What gives this poem unity is the sequence of the passing day framed within the images of the postman at dawn and nightfall, and the unity of the place Hamnavoe, seen in its apparent diversity through the recurrent images of gulls and boats and the sea. The four-line stanzas with their two long lines and two short lines, make a regular pattern that is completed by the additional short line in the last stanza.

Let us now consider the poem 'The Old Women'. The first noticeable thing about it is that it is divided into three sections. These help us to get into the theme. The first section contrasts the many moods of drunkenness with the single occupation of the old women, and the sweetness of the drunkard's pleasure with the bitterness of the women's displeasure. The second section, which is a typical piece of malicious gossip, follows the same theme of displeasure at the sight of pleasure and establishes the hereditary nature of the weakness for drink; the individual's straying from sober behaviour has been elevated into a transmitted vice, a sin of the fathers. So far the old women have been seen as upholders of virtue and respectability, expressing a Presbyterian morality. The third section changes the image of the old women after the first line, and they become the malicious enemies of goodness and sobriety, hardly able to disguise their delight at the death of the worthy young man. They have changed from gossiping bitches into chanting witches, from women into hags. This may suggest that George Mackay Brown is pointing to a closeness between a narrow-minded Calvinist 'goodness' and an evil-minded delight in other people's grief and death. The image of the hags weeping and gloating over the body lying dripping on the flag-stones does not seem to be a likely picture from from real life but is more of a symbolic posing of the elements of good and evil in a wordpainting that might remind us of a traditional religious subject in art – the women mourning over the body of Christ taken down from the Cross.

The second noticeable thing about 'The Old Women' is that the third section is longer than either of the first two, six lines as against four and four. As we saw, the first two sections were on the same theme and the third brought in a change. This turn in the thought is one of the characteristic features of the fourteen-line sonnet form, along with the patterns of rhymes that we find in the different sections. Thus George Mackay Brown has used a very traditional poetic form to make a savage comment about a particular traditional outlook on life in the local setting of his own Hamnavoe.

In both the poems we have looked at, the structure has been a vital part of the poem and a key to the understanding of it. Even in a very short poem like 'Unlucky Boat' we can see how structure controls the content to a considerable degree. There is a single introductory statement – 'The boat has killed three people' – followed by the accounts of the deaths. First there is Sib, the craftsman, whose death is treated with grim laconic humour. Second, there is Mansie, the fisherman, whose drowning in Scapa Flow is described in romantic terms (bar of silver under the moon', 'wands', 'put a spell', 'ushered . . . to meet the cold green angels'). Finally there is Angus, whose associations are with farming ('Dounby Market', 'barley stalk') and whose death is a foredoomed and harsh cutting-short of life. The poem is concluded by a personified vision of the boat as both accursed bitch and evil witch lurking among barren rocks of a sinister name, and by an epilogue in which the tinker outcasts of society ward off its evil with a traditional Catholic ritual gesture. The effect of this structure, finally, is to suggest that the different types in modern Orkney society are defenceless against malevolent forces; only those who are still in touch with the harmonious pre-Reformation past can evade them. The poem becomes more than just an anecdote about a boat; it becomes a patterned allegory of fate.

In 'The Hawk' the structure is very obvious; the poem is tightly held in the sequence of seven days with a 'stanza' of three lines to each. The pattern is a simple one – the day; the place where the hawk stoops from the sky; his intended prey (except on two days); the outcome of his swoop. During the week, the hawk is successful on three days, and the chicken, the blackbird and little Tom's rabbit fall prey to him. Twice the hawk is driven off – by the sheepdog protecting the lambs and by the rat – and on one day he is the object of the birdwatchers' solemn study. The week is, of course, a cycle of days and the hawk's end is shadowed in his beginning; the successful killing of the chicken at Bigging on Sunday is the reason for Jock's being ready for him with his gun on Saturday, and the hawk's final fall is of a different kind from the others. The relationship between the hawk and man is an ambiguous one. On the one hand, man helps to provide the hawk with some of his food, enabling him to lord over the chickens and rabbits on the crofts, and man studies him with some admiration. On the other hand, the hawk is overshadowed and dwarfed to 'a small wing' by man's power, both the silent power of man's binocular-enhanced vision and the blast of Jock's gun. Nature's power is not secure and the apparent dominance of the hawk is only at man's sufferance.

A careful look at 'Beachcomber' will reveal a structure and development of thought which are much the same as in 'The Hawk', although in this poem it is the beachcomber himself who speaks. His outlook on life is conveyed through what he tells us of his finds on the beach, his reactions to them and his dreams.

In 'Unlucky Boat' we found that the tinkers were people apart from the mainstream of the island community. Tinkers are common figures in George Mackay Brown's poems and stories. Often they are colourful preservers of old traditions, or of a more wholesome outlook on life than the respectable materialistic society that they live apart from and yet live off like parasites. Remember the tinker like 'a tartan gull' in 'Hamnavoe', free and wandering as the seabirds, but hanging round the doors for scraps of charity. The relationship between tinkers and the rest of society is a prickly one; sometimes there is respect and sympathy, more often there is suspicion and hostility. The poem, 'Ikey on the People of Hellya', explores these different relationships in terms of the tinker

Ikey's thoughts about particular inhabitants of this imaginary island. Again, as in 'Unlucky Boat', we have crofter-farmers, fisherman and tradesman representing the respectable community, and as in some of the other poems we have a 'catalogue' structure with the different characters clearly presented to us in Ikey's reflections. There is Rognvald, who is hard and hostile; Mansie, who is soft and over-generous; Gray, sly but superstitious like most fishermen; Merran, the descendant of a witch burned at the public execution ground, and unsympathetic to tinkers; Simpson, waging constant cruel war against the rabbits that the tinker relies on for food; and Jeems, who will see Ikey properly coffined after death just as he sees him properly clad in life. Through the poem can be seen Ikey's sly touches of humour as he suggests how he makes ends meet at the expense of some of them.

Another poem, 'Tinkers,' conveys the contradictory impressions of tinkers as both admirable and disreputable, rich princes and ragged paupers, alluringly magical and disappointingly squalid. Merran again appears, the descendant of the witch shut in to respectability like a caged bird of prey and seeming to envy the tinkers' magical freedom.

Tinkers

Three princes rigged like scarecrows
Straggled along the shore
And every clucking wife
Ran in and barred her door.

Their coats hung in such shreds
The dogs barked as they came.
O but their steps were a dance,
Their eyes all black flame!

The wife's undone her pack
And spread it at our door.

Grails, emeralds, peacock feathers
Scattered over the floor.

The man flashed his bow,
His fiddle had only one string,
But where is the sun-drowned lark
Like that can sing?

The dark boy wore his rags
Like an April-awakened tree,
Or as a drift of seaweed
Glitters on the arms of the sea.

Princes, they ruled in our street
A long shining age,
While Merran peeped through her curtains
Like a hawk from a cage.

Paupers, they filthied our pier
A piece of one afternoon,
Then scowled, stank, shouldered their packs
And cursed and were gone.

In 'A Warped Boat' there is another important influence
at work. Death by water has figured in many of the
poems we have looked at. In 'Hamnavoe' to begin with,
there was the 'grief by the shrouded nets'; then we had
the old women moaning joyfully over the 'body dripping
on the stones' the unlucky boat ushering Mansie 'to meet
the cold green angels' of the sea, 'the Danish wreck', 'the
Spanish ship wrecked at the Kame' and the 'seaman's
skull with sand spilling out'. It seems that where there is
grief, it is the business of women. The attitude of the
fishermen themselves is more fatalistic. In 'A Warped
Boat', we have the clearest expression of this understated
acceptance of death. When his open boat reveals its
weakness and is about to sink in the swell, Willag utters
his last instructions and his grimly humorous exit lines in
the reflective contented tone of the crofter contemplating a

good harvest and a fine brew. Of course, this is not a realistic situation. The distance between Willag and the watchers on the shore would rule out the quiet tone. What we have is an artistically contrived or heightened death of the kind that will be found described in the Norse sagas. The warrior-farmers of the heroic Viking age were given such laconic humorous last words by the saga-makers of Norway and Iceland, and George Mackay Brown sees Willag as being in this mould, disposing of his beasts, joking about his wife's disapproval of his drinking and wryly comparing the salt water to his usual evening refreshment before he goes under. Structurally, the poem is very simple, based on the grammatical construction:– 'As one would say . . . So Willag . . . rose . . . and remarked.' The line, 'His seaboots filled and Willag said no more' implies the drowning rather than states it.

This poem is part of George Mackay Brown's poem cycle, *Fisherman With Ploughs*. In this long sequence of poems, we see the valley of Rackwick on the island of Hoy through the ages from the first Norse settlement through the conversion to Christianity and Presbyterian Reformation to the modern age and beyond. 'A Warped Boat' comes from the section called 'Foldings', in which Death is a prominent subject. Slowly the valley moves into decline until the crofts are deserted. Here is the poem that ends the section, showing the valley in its final empty and ruined state. Each named croft is shown in terms of an image of desolation and reference to the dead cold hearth that was once the focus of warmth and life.

Dead Fires

At Burnmouth the door hangs from a broken hinge
And the fire is out.

The windows of Shore empty sockets
And the hearth coldness.

At Bunertoon the small drains are choked.
Thrushes sing in the chimney.

Stars shine through the roofbeams of Scar.
No flame is needed
To warm ghost and nettle and rat.

Greenhill is sunk in a new bog.
No kneeling woman
Blows red wind through squares of ancient turf.

The Moss is a tumble of stones.
That one black stone
Is the stone where the hearth fire was rooted.

In Crawnest the sunken hearth
Was an altar for priests of legend,
Old seamen from the clippers with silken beards.

The three-toed pot at the wall of Park
Is lost to woman's cunning.
A slow fire of rust eats the cold iron.

The sheep drift through Reumin all winter.
Sheep and snow
Blanch fleetingly the black stone.

From that sacred stone the children of the valley
Drifted lovewards
And out of labour to the lettered kirkyard stone.

The fire beat like a heart in each house
From the first cornerstone
Till they led through a sagging lintel the last old one.

The poor and the good fires are all quenched.
Now, cold angel, keep the valley
From the bedlam and cinders of A Black Pentecost.

The 'cold angel' of the last stanza is the sea, as in 'Unlucky Boat', here seen as a protector of the islands from the devastating power of 'Progress'. The final image of the poem is of the nuclear holocaust that George Mackay Brown sees as the ultimate blasphemy of a materialistic age, obsessed by scienfitic progress at the expense of traditional values. The last part of *Fishermen With Ploughs* deals with the aftermath of the nuclear destruction when survivors drift over the sea to the remote deserted island valley to found a new settlement and begin a new cycle of social development.

It should be clear now from the poems that we have been studying that George Mackay Brown is doing a number of things very skilfully indeed. As mentioned at the beginning, he is celebrating his own homeland of Orkney, particularly as it was in the past, and is presenting us with a wealth of vivid characters and incidents and pictures. Yet there is much more in his poetry. As we have seen, there is a highly organised structure in nearly every poem that controls the content and helps to concentrate its impact on the reader and heighten the power of the poem's ideas. And there are ideas in plenty in the poems. Within the Orkney setting George Mackay Brown reveals and develops his concerns in wider areas of human thought and feeling. We have seen a joy in the rich diversity of a way of life that has grown slowly out of a continuing tradition in one place. A condemnation of the narrow life-denying outlook that confuses morality with a hatred of life's pleasures, a sense of the precariousness of life in the face of chance and fate. Also an awareness of man's power and potential irresponsibility exercised over both Nature and his own social achievements, and a regret that, in turning away from a secure faith and tradition towards material progress and scientific discovery, man is losing much that made life most satisfying. Many people may find George Mackay Brown too inclined to turn his back on the modern world and its often harsh reality, but there is no denying that he has created a coherent poetic world of colour and image and character that can give great satisfaction. It is a real world heightened by imagination, and its values are basic ones, clarified by being put into a simpler context than the world that most of us inhabit.

13. Edwin Morgan
by
JOHN BLACKBURN

(*The assistance of Fred Gibbons, Depute Headmaster of Garrion Academy, in the preparation of this essay is greatfully acknowledged.*)

Edwin Morgan is best known, in schools at least, for what are termed his Glasgow poems. These poems, however, do not represent anything like the range of Morgan's work, and the opportunity afforded by this present volume to offer a wider view of his poetic output is welcome.

There are two difficulties which, it seems to me, must face anyone writing a short piece on the poetry of Edwin Morgan. First, there is the exceptional amount of variety to be found in the work. Somehow this has to be encompassed. Then there is the difficulty that some readers may not consider that what they see on the page in front of them is poetry at all!

It is certainly true that a good deal of Morgan's earlier writing may be too explicit, too full and plain in its statement, to allow the reader room to imagine for himself what the 'poem' is about – and that kind of freedom is *usually* regarded as being part and parcel of the experience of reading poetry. Then, too, for some there may be insufficient feel of the *sound* of language in the lines, the flow and echo of the words which traditionally characterise poetry. Whatever one thinks about these things, it is to be stressed that not only poems make for good or interesting writing! There are other sorts of good writing besides what is traditionally thought of as poetry – maybe some which have not even been dreamed of as yet! Morgan has always been prominent among those willing to try new forms and new ways of expression, on the page and in the ear.

Let us turn now to survey the variety of Morgan's work. All the poems to which reference is made in the following pages are to be found in the recently published *Poems of Thirty Years*.

The first collection which established Morgan, among a wide readership, was *The Second Life* (1968). It was a remarkably varied collection. It began with three poems about well-known people, Marilyn Monroe, Edith Piaf and Ernest Hemingway.* The poems about the women display that breathless, spasmodic style, which was common in Morgan's earlier work, where short statement follows short statement, short question follows short question and where the reader is left asking himself about the difference between prose and poetry.

Let no one say communication is cantword.
They had to lift her hand from the bedside telephone.

The Hemingway Poem, 'The Old Man and the Sea' is different. It is, I think the first poem in which the style

---

* One of Morgan's common practices is to write poems based upon news items rather than upon his immediate experience.

of the American poets in whom Morgan is interested
(poets like Carlos Williams), is apparent in his work.

> And a white mist rolled out of the Pacific
> and crept over the sand, stirring nothing –
> cold, cold as nothing is cold
> on those living highways, moved in
> over the early morning trucks,
> chilling the drivers in their cabins. . .

The poem is about Hemingway's suicide and it ends in
that open, questioning manner which is characteristic of
Morgan.

> fumbling nothing, but leaving questions
> that echo beyond Spain and Africa.
> Questions, not answers, chill the heart here,
> a chained dog whining in the straw,
> the gunsmoke marrying the sea-mist,
> the silence of the inhuman valleys.

Not long after these poems come the Glasgow ones, the
ones selected for *Gallery*. One of these, 'In the Snack-bar'
seems to have become for Morgan what 'The Lake Isle of
Innisfree' was for Yeats, the poem which dogs the foot-
steps of its writer. In the first part of this poem an old,
blind, hunchbacked man is shown, intruding into the
lives of those around him in the snack-bar, by knocking
over a cup and asking to go to the toilet. In the second,
slow, section of the poem, the writer takes him there,
across the floor, down the stairs, into the toilet, and then
up the stairs, across the floor and out of the door to
where he is helped on to a bus, he having nothing else
to do but 'haul his blind hump through these rains of
August'. 'In the Snack-bar' is a moving, 'realistic' piece
of description; it is one of Morgan's 'camera' poems,
where the focus shifts, narrowing and widening as it
goes, but it is not, I think, among the best of his work. The
weakness, for me, lies just here and there, in the more

general statements and comments which Morgan allows himself. What for example, of the claim that it is the 'persisting patience of the undefeated' that is the nature of man?

'King Billy' is a less straightforward statement: there is more one can read into it in terms of irony and allusion and the use of imagery. The opening is cold, grey and heavy, the scene in the graveyard lit by the uncertain, 'flickering' light of the streetlamps. There is a restlessness in the images: they are not constant. The wreath, too, is blown from its place on the grave of the hero of former times, whose name, Billy, echoes the name of King William of Orange. The funeral procession (in the second section) of the hero of thirty years ago who died an old man, alone, in a box bed, is viewed ironically – it being noted at the same time that there is no irony felt among the mourners as they bear the violent gang-leader to his grave to the sound of 'Onward Christian Soldiers'. These people seem indifferent to the memories of the violence perpetrated by King Billy in his sherrickings (verbal abuses) and his slashings, until he, along with the others of his type, was obliged to scuff his razors down the street drains to avoid the wrath of the Law, in the form of Lord Sillitoe whose determined attack upon gang violence became part of Glasgow's history. The poem ends with an exhortation to

Deplore what is to be deplored,
and then find out the rest.

Whatever doubts some may have about the classification of these pieces (prose-poems?) and about the exhortations and exclamations to be found in them, there can be little doubt that they do capture *remarkably* well, as does 'Good Friday', the 'feel' of the life from which they emerge. Another such piece from *The Second Life* is 'Glasgow Green'. It is a stark poem, the central event of which is a homosexual attack in the park which lies in the centre of Glasgow, bordering the River Clyde. Crichton

Smith has praised this poem highly for its harsh uncompromising presentation of, and comment on life around the Green. Even more stark and startling, I think, is the longer poem 'Stobhill', which is to be found in the collection *From Glasgow to Saturn*. Stobhill is the name of a hospital in Glasgow and the poem is about the destruction of the aborted foetus of a live child. The various people involved in the drama, the doctor, the boilerman, the mother, the father and the hospital porter each make a speech, as if to a court, telling what they know of the relevant events and explaining why they acted as they did. The court in question is a court of law, but that is not made prominent in the poem: the court could just as well be the court of humankind. The explanations reveal a tangle of weakness and selfishness; such common decency as emerges only serves to emphasise the horror of the situation.

'Trio' is a poem at the other end of the emotional range altogether. In it three young people, 'a young man and two girls, under the Christmas lights –' scatter back with their laughter and colour and love the 'Monsters of the year', the dark memories of, and perhaps forebodings about, those parts of the year which lie beyond this moment 'at the end of his winter's day.'

In *Gnomes*, published in 1979, there appeared creations of a different and relatively novel sort – concrete poems. These are pieces in which the lay-out of the 'words' on the page plays a very obvious part in the total effect of the poem. Morgan is one of the best known exponents of concrete poetry. His pieces are characterised by a sense of the frustrations and limitations which inhabit the lives of most of us. The tone is genial and comic, just as it is in many of his other kinds of lighter poems. It is worth noting in passing, however, that poetry which is laid out in unusual ways on the page need not always be light poetry. A look at some of the poems of Carlos Williams, upon which Morgan himself makes comment elsewhere in this book, will convince the reader of that.

busybykeobloodybizzinbees
bloodybusybykeobizzinbees
bizzinbloodybykeobusybees
busybloodybykeobizzinbees
bloodybykeobusybizzinbees
bizzinbykeobloodybusybees
busybykeobizzinbloodybees
bloodybykeobizzinbusybees
bizzinbusybykeobloodybees
busybizzinbykeobloodybees
bloodybizzinbykeobusybees
bizzinbusybloodybykeobees

O Pioneers!

THIS TUNNEL WAS BUGN BEGUBNUGN IN 1880
WILLIAM SHARP

Workman's inscription on entrance to abandoned
Channel Tunnel at Dover

Channel Tunnel bugn.
1880. Sharp Wilgn.

Tannel Chunnel begum.
8018. Shart Willum.

Tennal Chennul gbung.
8081. Shant Willung.

Chennal Tennal bengug.
8108. Shunt Willibug.

Chunnal Tennel begbugn.
8801. Slunt Willubugmn.

Chuntenlannel begubnugn.
8810. Blunt Wuglbumlugn.

+ + + + + + + + + + + +

10880. Brigde bugn.

Even the computer in another of Morgan's concrete poems, 'The Computer's First Christmas Card', can only do its best, starting with Christmas and ending up stuttering its way towards chrysanthemums.

Towards the end of *The Second Life* there appears a major poem in Morgan's work, 'In Sobieski's Shield'. Morgan believes that, despite what some social theorists and political economists have to say, quite properly it may be, about the dangers and undesirabilities inherent in many forms of scientific and technological development, the fact remains that such development will take place and that we will soon live in a very technological environment. This being so, poetry, he argues, must not become disengaged from technological matters. The poet must carry human values into the world of future science and technology.

In the poem 'In Sobieski's Shield', a man who has been beamed up from Earth to a minor planet of a sun in Sobieski's Shield, takes stock of the situation, noting that he has come out of the beaming quite well, having lost only one finger and acquired only a strange twinge in a kneecap. His wife, in her new, second life, finds herself with a beautiful crown of bright red hair and his son has gained the deep voice of manhood. These are images of vitality and hope. Hope too is implied in the man's awareness that he has left behind the old world of shell holes and war – a memory revived in him by the sight of a lake of mercury. The poem, written without sentence divisions or marked pauses, except between the sections, ends with the family stepping out to the life that lies before them.

> . . . let's take our second
> like our first life out from the dome are the suits
> ready the mineral storm is quieter it's hard
> to go let's go

Morgan's interest in technology does not always lead him to look forward to new worlds. In the poem 'From the

Domain of Arnheim', he imagines people from an 'advanced' society visiting by means of a time ship people in a primitive society and bringing back from the visit 'deeper sourvenirs' than any 'rocks or seeds', bringing that is memories of the people of Arnheim living positive, human lives, untroubled by fear of gods or strangers. Nor are his planetary poems always serious in tone. In *From Glasgow to Saturn*, there is 'The First Men on Mercury', a dialogue between men from Earth and some of the inhabitants of Mercury. As they talk they struggle (as William Sharp and the computer did) to express meaning in their respective languages – and the Mercury men end speaking cold, clear English while the men from Earth, ordered to return home immediately by their 'hosts' can only exclaim in horror,

Stretterworra gawl, gawl . . .

In *The New Divan*, 1977, are some of Morgan's most poised poems. Number 40 in this series takes us back to Morgan's darker poetry.

Given a gerbil, the child strokes its fur.
It struggles – oh how anxious it is! Out or in,
it trusts a cage more than love, that like wax
can melt to fearful shapes and suffocate. Red
from a painting-session varicoses her arms
like a murderer's – or something,
the gerbil doesn't know, but sniffs and strains, and
with a slap she returns it to the cage. Parents pronounce
bed, where her little rage of rejection will swell,
rooted in darkness. The heart is dark and broad,
and twisted like an araucaria under
a varicose sky. Lamp, coffee, cigarette
are innocently sweet; workbox, divan.

This sense of inner darkness, of evil, is more

pronounced in these later poems than in any of Morgan's earlier work.

One of the most relentless poems in this darker, more violent kind is 'Iran', from the *Uncollected Poems*.

Iran

Tip the second lorry-load – the adultress is still
    groaning.
What sort of stones are these, for the love of Allah?
Is it pumice? There is only a trickle of blood.
She is actually moving, either her arms or her legs
cannot have been broken. Such a corps of bunglers
I have never, not ever, seen, even in the north.
Are you saboteurs, and of morality too?
Look at that: an arm sticking through the pile,
    making a fist, of all things, not fingers
stretched in the sort of appeal your feint-heart Christ-
    lot
would fall for! Let her fist be rock-hard,
we have harder rocks to rain on her from quarries
as bottomless as her iniquities.
Tip it! Tip it on her! Right. Let her think of lovers
of stone alone, stone breath and brawn
to press those speaking peaks of breasts to rubble
and make her girdle redder than a rose.
You fools, the fist! The fist still shows!

There is much in this which makes it an intense poem: anger, irony, the urgent, excited movement of the speaking voice; the use of alliteration, on the strong letter b and the impatient sounding f. The playing-off of one type of image against another, the images of suffering flesh on the one hand and those of stone and rubble on the other. And the tight, almost shockingly abrupt nature of the piece where we are taken right in to the event, not at its beginning but at the second lorry-load and then ejected

141

from it again while the fist still shows, while the job is still not over with. 'Iran' works successfully both as a protest and as a poem.

Morgan, then, is a writer who is quite deliberately pushing poetry in what he regards as forward directions, in terms of language, form and subject matter. Sometimes comic, sometimes serious, sometimes urgently serious, he seems never to depart for long from the idea that poetry has a role to play in people's lives and in a changing society. For him the writing of poetry has been, I think, as it has also been for Crichton Smith, a long, thoughtful, journey from over thirty years back to the present time. Among his latest poems is one about a trapeze artist and juggler, 'Cinquevalli'. Morgan himself favours this poem. I imagine he does so because Cinquevalli, that man of immense poise and determination, is an embodiment of the accomplishment, and humanity and humour which are at the heart of his own large and influential body of poetry.

Cinquevalli

Cinquevalli is falling, falling.
The shining trapeze kicks and flirts free,
solo performer at last.
The sawdust puffs up with a thump,
settles on a tangle of broken limbs.
St Petersburg screams and leans.
His pulse flickers with the gas-jets. He lives.

Cinquevalli has a therapy.
In his hospital bed, in his hospital chair
he holds a ball, lightly, lets it roll round his hand,
or grips it tight, gauging its weight and resistance,
begins to balance it to feel its life attached to his
by will and knowledge, invisible strings
that only he can see. He throws it
from hand to hand, always different,

142

always the same, always
different, always the
same.
His muscles learn to think, his arms grow very strong.

Cinquevalli in sepia
looks at me from an old postcard: bundle of enigmas.
Half faun, half military man; almond eyes, curly hair,
conventional moustache; tights, and a tunic loaded
with embroideries, tassels, chains, fringes; hand on hip
with a large signet-ring winking at the camera
but a bull neck and shoulders and a cannon-ball
at his elbow as he stands by the posing pedestal;
half reluctant, half truculent,
half handsome, half absurd,
but let me see you forget him: not to be done.

Cinquevalli is a juggler.
In a thousand theatres, in every continent,
he is the best, the greatest. After eight years
    perfecting
he can balance one billiard ball on another billiard ball
on top of a cue on top of a third billiard ball
in a wine-glass held in his mouth. To those
who say the balls are waxed, or flattened,
he patiently explains the trick will only work
because the spheres are absolutely true.
There is no deception in him. He is true.

Cinquevalli is juggling with a bowler,
a walking-stick, a cigar, and a coin.
Who foresees? How to please.
The last time round, the bowler
flies to his head, the stick sticks in his hand,
the cigar jumps into his mouth, the coin
lands on his foot – ah, but
is kicked into his eye
and held there as the miraculous monocle
without which the portrait would be incomplete.

Cinquevalli is practising.
He sits in his dressing-room talking to some friends,
at the same time writing a letter with one hand
and with the other juggling four balls.
His friends think of demons, but
'You could all do this,' he says,
sealing the letter with a billiard ball.

Cinquevalli is on the high wire in Odessa.
The roof cracks, he is falling, falling
into the audience, a woman breaks his fall,
he cracks her like a flea, but lives.

Cinquevalli broods in his armchair in Brixton Road.
He reads in the paper about the shells whining
at Passchendaele, imagines the mud and the dead.
He goes to the window and wonders through that dark
    evening
what is happening in Poland where he was born.
His neighbours call him a German spy.
'Kestner, Paul Kestner, that's his name!'
'Keep Kestner out of the British music-hall!'
He frowns; it is cold; his fingers seem stiff and old.

Cinquevalli tosses up a plate of soup
and twirls it on his forefinger; not a drop spills.
He laughs, and well may he laugh
who can do that. The astonished table
breathe again, laugh too, think the world
a spinning thing that spills, for a moment, no drop.

Cinquevalli's coffin sways through Brixton
only a few months before the Armistice.
Like some trick they cannot get off the ground
it seems to burden the shuffling bearers, all their arms
cross-juggle that displaced person, that man
of balance, of strength, of delights and marvels,
in his unsteady box at last into the earth.

14. The Gaelic Tradition

(A Prologue to translations from Gaelic of poems by Derick Thomson)

There was a time when Gaelic was the language of Scotland. It is still one of the languages of a considerable part of Scotland, the Highlands and Islands, and in our time, from the 1930s onward, there have emerged from the lands of the Gael a number of accomplished poets. Their poetry, in translation, although it comes from a tradition which is very different from that of modern English poetry, is not particularly difficult to understand, provided one has some knowledge of the Gaelic tradition and of the events to which reference is made, directly or indirectly, in many of the poems

Accordingly, before surveying the poems of Derick Thomson, who is one of these contemporary Gaelic poets and who is also Professor of Celtic at Glasgow University, it seems obvious that we should take a look, however brief, at the history of the Scottish Gael and the sorts of poetry that were part of it.*

About the beginning of the sixth century AD, in the country now called Scotland, but then known as Alba, Gaelic was established as the chief language of the people. It had been brought to Alba by colonists from Ireland, the Scots. The language flourished throughout Scotland for nearly six centuries and then began gradually to be forced, by the growth of Anglo-Saxon influence in the south-east of the country, up into the remoter areas of the north and west. There it continued in use, as the language of the defeated Gael, the second-class citizen who had been turned away from the centre of power.

As the Scottish Gaels settled into their mountainous and loch-divided lands in the north and west they, and their poetry, became more self-enclosed, separated from the culture of Europe and from that of Lowland Scotland

* Much of what is recorded here will also serve as a background to the poetry of Iain Crichton Smith.

and even from that of their fellow Gaels in Ireland. Much of the early poetry was made by bards who belonged to, or served, particular clans. These bards recited the praises of the chiefs and of the clans, part of the purpose of this being to help to maintain the morale and the social values of the clan and of the culture within which the clan existed. The praise was usually lavish, hyperbolic: there was no point in being modest in such circumstances. Often in such praise poems there would be mention of the ancestors of the hero, the genealogy of the clan. The bards engaged, too, in poems of energetic abuse of the enemies of the clan, poems full of invective and dispraise. Bardic poetry was what Donald MacAulay has called a poetry of 'celebration and participation'.

Not all bardic poetry, however, was in praise of chief or clan. There is to be found also in the bardic tradition what is called courtly love poetry. Although this was written in the formal style of the bards, strong, personal feeling is to be found in it, as in poems like Niall Mor MacMhuirich's well-known and beautiful 'Farewell for ever to last night' where the only apparently formal gesture is in the last verse where the poet appeals to 'Mother Mary of fostering grace'. In translation:

Farewell for ever to last night;
swift though it passed, its joy remains:
though I were hanged for my share in it
I'd live it over tonight again.

There are two in this house tonight
whose eyes give their secrets away:
though they are not lip to lip
eager is the eyes' play.

The eyes' swift glances must give all
the tale their prisoned lips would tell;
the eyes have kept no secret here,
lips' silence is of no avail

Those who would make my true words false,
have sealed my lips, O languid eye;
but in your corner, out of reach,
understand what my eyes say:

"Keep the memory of this night,
let there be no change till doom;
do not let the morning in:
throw out the cold day from the room."

Mother Mary, of fostering grace,
since poets look to you for light,
save me now, and take my hand –
farewell for ever to last night.

This poem, sometimes known as 'The Message of the
Eyes', is part of the poetry of the society, the refined society of the time. But besides this relatively formal, bardic
type verse, there were songs too, composed by different
types of people, from the sixteenth century onwards particularly. These were on the subjects one would expect
– love, disappointment in love, bereavement, hunting,
work of various kinds. . . . Such songs were full of activity and physical sensation, and passions of love, and
hate.

Would, O God, that she would come,
with her hand wounded and her leg broken,
seeking a leech at the side of every bed,
and no leech in the land but me;
by my hand I would take courage,
I would bend bone and draw blood;
when I closed your coffin lid
I would put earth on the bank of your tomb.

So run some of the lines of a woman's jealousy poem. At
the other extreme there are these beautiful lines from a
love poem.

You took the east from me, you took the west,
you took the moon from me, the sun above,
you took the heart from me, from out my breast,
you almost took my God from me, white love."

From the seventeenth century onwards, pressures mounted against this Gaelic culture. As the economy and 'civilisation' and power of the South grew, the inhabitants thereof became less and less inclined to tolerate the Gael's tendency to descend upon them in raids for cattle and other goods which he needed to sustain his own bare economy among the mountains and moorlands of the north. The citizens of the south then were, for the main part, relieved when, after the massive defeat of the Jacobite clans at Culloden in 1745, General Wade with his roads and 'Butcher' Cumberland with his troops continued the suppression of the clans and drove the surviving chiefs into exile.

During these troubled, sometimes desperate, times remarkable poets are to be found, surprising though that may seem. In the seventeenth century, there was Iain Lom (the sharp one) directing his 'intellectual shrapnel' against the movement of power to the south and in the eighteenth century there was Alexander MacDonald writing nature poems and clever political satires. And there was Rob Donn in far north Sutherland writing love poems and satires and nature poems and elegies. Near Bridge of Orchy in Argyll there was Duncan Ban MacIntyre, Fair Duncan of the Songs, unable to read or write, but creating still in the oral tradition some of the best known of all the Gaelic songs and poems. His 'In Praise of Ben Dorain' is to my ears, and they are not Gaelic ones, one of the grandest and most skillfully made of all poemsongs. MacIntyre follows the movement, the structure, of the pibroch, the 'big' music of the pipes, as he describes in detail and with delight the mountain Ben Dorain and the life of the deer upon it. And there was, too, William Ross who died at the age of twenty eight leaving behind some of the liveliest and most passionate of Gaelic love poetry.

> Oh would that you and I
> were alone in a room together,
> and that for all the seven days of the seven years.
> And that the door were made of iron
> and it locked
> and the keys lost
> and the blind looking for them.

It is interesting to note how the modern poets, Sorley MacLean and Iain Crichton Smith and Derick Thomson all address William Ross in their poetry, seeming to sense in him a kindred spirit to their own.

In the eighteenth century, then, Gaelic poetry flourished, even though Gaeldom itself was going through what would now, I suppose, be described as a 'traumatic' time. But no poets to equal these men of the eighteenth century are to be found in the following one. By the nineteenth century the close bonds between chief and clan, which had been a vital part of the tradition, had been broken, destroyed by the 1745 rebellion and its aftermath. The new 'chiefs', the new landowners, saw that there was more profit to be made from sheep than from tenant crofters. Consequently, the people in many areas of the Highlands were forced from their lands to make way for the sheep. Some went to the south, in search of a living in the developing towns; many went abroad, mainly to Canada, being taken there, in many instances, in the ships which had brought cattle from Canada to the markets in Britain. There was no joy in these departures, no sense of willingness and adventure. The people were leaving lands and homes and kinships which had been the very stuff of their lives, the means by which they identified themselves as communities and even as individuals. These Clearances, as they were called, were a time of real desolation and heartbreak in the Highlands.

Moreover, with the Clearances there came another major development, some would say another major desolation, in the Highlands – Calvinism. (A description of this form of Christianity is to be found near the beginning of the chapter on Iain Crichton Smith's poetry.) The broken people seemed to find a refuge from their troubles in their increased commitment to Calvinism with its powerful emotional demands and its pointing of the mind away from the things of this earth and towards the things of the great hereafter. Even the loss of land and house and community were of relative unimportance when compared with the fear of Hellfire and the hope of salvation. Preaching which could work the congregation to a pitch of fear and excitement was looked for and ministers who could not produce this were, as Iain Crichton Smith once remarked, even in the twentieth century referred to as 'wooden ministers'.

The effects of the Clearances and the fervour of Calvinistic belief seemed to leave little room for poetry, at least for poetry of power and wit and skill. We find instead sentimental verse, homesick and very local, dominating the scene. And the Education Act of 1872 did nothing to help the situation. It demanded that all children in Britain, whatever their native language might be, should be taught in English. It's not difficult to imagine the handicap which that created for any bright Gaelic youngster trying to feel his way into life and learning. Moreover, the attempts to help the situation by providing simple textbooks served to reinforce the myth that the recipients were simple-minded people! The nineteenth century was a bad one for the old traditions, and it is to the events of that century – the Clearances, the upsurge of Calvinism and the attack upon Gaelic language and culture – that one finds reference being often made in the poetry of Derick Thomson.

The early part of the twentieth century was not much different from the nineteenth as far as poetry was concerned. Then came a sudden revival, the main thrust of which began in the thirties and forties.

The new, modern, Gaelic poets, though still deeply rooted in their native culture, are, in the main, highly educated men who have moved outside of their tradition and are able to see it in new perspectives. Their comment upon it is widely informed, sometimes disapproving. Besides, the writing of these modern poets is not, as nearly all the earlier poetry was, exclusively about Gaeldom and the life therein. They are involved with matters elsewhere in the world. Such a widening of interest and theme is, of course, to be expected. Given the nature of our times, the development of media and communications, the involvement of peoples with one another in a 'shrinking' world, there would be something strange and unhealthy about a culture whose intelligentsia stayed firmly rooted within it. So, in his poem 'Going Home', for example, we find Iain Crichton Smith telling how he will go home to his island, trying to forget the world he is leaving behind him. But that world will not be forgotten, that 'great fire at the back of our thoughts', Nagasaki and Hiroshima. And again, in one of the best of the poems about the Second World War, 'Bizerta', by George Campbell Hay, we have the image of another fire, that of the burning town of Bizerta in North Africa where the flames dart up and swell and decline and leap up in throbs and seem like a heart, a pulse of evil in the night sky.

The same sort of involvement in matters beyond the homeland is to be seen in the war poetry of Sorley MacLean, a major figure in twentieth-century Gaelic poetry.

Much of MacLean's poetry is, however, more inward looking, to himself and to his Gaelic background. He has written, for example, what for the twentieth century is an astonishing praise poem, an elegy for his brother Calum Iain MacLean. It is a poem rooted in place and genealogy. His poetry is, too, often complex, both in terms of the feelings involved and in terms of the imagery and symbolism used.

Although MacLean's poetry has received much attention, it seemed to me, when compiling *Gallery*, that modern Gaelic poetry would be best introduced to English-speaking readers through the work not of MacLean but of another of the principal Gaelic poets of the twentieth century, Derick Thomson. One of the characteristics of Thomson's writing is that it is fairly easy to grasp at a first reading; it is easy to follow the images through and to see what the poem is 'about'. Then, the more you look, the more you see in the poem. And that, I thought, made it a very suitable kind of poetry through which to contact a culture in many ways different from one's own.

Thomson's poetry, like that of the tradition which lies behind it, is full of anger and love, praise and dispraise. His readings of it, unlike those of MacLean, are not reminiscent of the recitations of the bards or of the style of Yeats. They are rather, precise and thoughtful, though when it comes to poems like 'Coffins' and 'Strathnaver' and 'The Scarecrow', the reading acquires a kind of whispering intensity that lifts the lines off the page altogether. They seem to come then, like his own Catriona Mhor's cleverness-with-words, 'from the heart of the race'.

Here then is part of an edited transcript of a conversation between Derick Thomson and myself about some of his shorter poems, for we could not afford in the circumstances to tackle the longer poems or the sequences such as 'The Plough' or 'The Ark of the Covenant.'

15. Derick Thomson

in conversation with
JOHN BLACKBURN

(Transcript of a conversation)

BLACKBURN: I think that one of the most obvious things about your poetry is that it is rooted in your native island, Lewis.

THOMSON: That's certainly the case. So much so that some readers think that this is an obsessive interest. I wouldn't quarrel too much with that because obsessions are, after all, an important aspect of our living, certainly an important aspect of a writer's work. I do remember becoming extremely interested in archaic and primitive features of life in Lewis. This was when I was quite a young fellow, in my twenties, and for some time after I had a fairly conscious wish to record these features and to reflect on them. I'm thinking particularly of the kind of life you got on rural Lewis in the 1920s and 1930s, before the great divide of the Second World War. So I think partly what I've been doing in my poems, sometimes involuntarily and sometimes in a more calculated way, is recording these impressions.

BLACKBURN: We should make the point here that these

poems were written in Gaelic, so that what we have in *Gallery* are not poems as they were first created, but translations of poems, English versions – and of course it is very, very difficult to translate a poem without losing a lot from it. You tend always to lose shades of meaning, allusions to things known only in the culture and language of the original poem, kinds of emotion even, that belong to one way of life and not to another. And the rhythm and flow of a language is nearly always lost in translation, though I know that you in fact take unusual care to preserve these as well as you can in your translations of your poems.

Well, can we turn to the poems? One of the simplest about your early experiences in Lewis is in *Gallery*, the poem 'Hands'. I think it's fairly easy to see what you're doing in this one, distinguishing between those which are of relatively little importance as you look back on them and those more valued, which were close to the life on the land and on the sea around Lewis.

But another poem which is built round memories of early days on Lewis is 'Catriona Mhòr', a rather more difficult poem perhaps for the outsider to understand altogether, without some comment.

THOMSON: This is a poem about a very picturesque and forceful character who is in the course of the poem made into something of a symbol. She's a symbol of the old Gaelic world, a very positive personality. So, although naturally she doesn't form part of my everyday thinking as I'm going about my normal tasks, her image is so positive that it doesn't become dimmed by time,

Catriona Mhòr
[*Big Catherine*].

Your picture is at the back of my mind
undimmed,
steady, set
among the broken images,
amid the movements,
untouched by age except the age you were,
the great round of the face like a clock
    stopped
on a Spring morning,
keeping me to the village time
with that wisdom
that flourished without books,
with the fun, the cleverness-with-words
that leapt from the heart of the race
before it was encased,
before it had the new valve in it
to keep it going in the new world.
That is the key to my museum,
the record on which I play my folklore,
the trowel with which I turn the ground
of the age that is now gone,
the image that keeps control over false
    images.

BLACKBURN: What I notice about the image of the woman
in the poem is that it has two different elements in it. At first you get the picture of an
old, or at least elderly, woman: she is 'steady,
set' and has lived for some time, 'untouched
by age'. The 'great round of the face' too suggests a person who has grown big, grown
slowly to be big. Yet, associated with her, in
the lines that follow, are things that imply
youth and vigour – Spring and flourishing.
And the cleverness-with-words leaps – leaps,
again a word that suggests vitality.

THOMSON: Yes, the sense of vitality is completely essential to the picture of her. Her vitality had something to do with how deeply she was steeped in the tradition, in the verbal tradition for example, in the tradition of wit, of storytelling, that sort of thing. She is a symbol of ancient wisdom, ancient practices but carrying that vitality right into our own times.

BLACKBURN: She reminds me of the two important figures in Celtic mythology, the Spring Maiden, who presided over that part of the year when things grew and flourished, from May to October, and the Winter Hag, who presided over the time of coldness and darkness and dearth and death. But as I understand her, the Winter Hag was not merely a figure associated with misery and hardship in an entirely negative way. She embodied wisdom; she reminded men of their mortality and of the pain inherent in living. Well, to me, Catriona Mhòr has something of both of these mythological figures in her.

THOMSON: Yes. I suppose any character of great vitality does embody both.

BLACKBURN: Can I ask you about one or two things in this poem? Am I right in thinking that 'the village time' refers to the ways of the village, the rhythms of village life?

THOMSON: That's right, yes. Keeping me right. It's a literal translation of a Gaelic idiom. In Gaelic it would make its point immediately whereas in English it perhaps needs a bit of explanation.

BLACKBURN: And then, a little later, we have talk of the heart and of the race being encased, having a new valve put in it, to make it suitable for the new world. The images are now cramping and unnatural.

THOMSON: Yes, this is to do with all the intrusions on ancient values and ancient ways of doing things and looking at things.

BLACKBURN: And then the last lines, with the keys and the record and the trowel. . . . .

THOMSON: These are all images of conservation and re-cording of traditions. But very often when you come to that stage, necessary though it is, the vital tradition is on the way out; it's practically gone. The trowel of the archaeol-ogist is not going to revive it.

BLACKBURN: But at the end we come back to the strong image of Catriona Mhòr, her picture at the back of your mind, 'the image that keeps con-trol over false images'. It's perhaps worth mentioning here that the figure of the old woman, or the mature mother-figure, is a very common one in modern Gaelic poetry, and indeed in Celtic writing. There are, for instance, all those Old Woman poems which appear in Iain Crichton Smith's work. And in his novel, *Consider the Lilies*, it's an old woman who is at the centre of the book, the subject of the book indeed. Then, over in Ire-land, there are the old women in the plays of Synge and there's Yeats calling Ireland itself an old Woman and there are the women, the mature women, of O'Casey's plays.

THOMSON: Yes, I think that women played an extremely important part in Gaelic society. And this is true if you go right back to old Irish times, the old Irish sagas. They play a very important part there too, you know. And there are a lot of very sharply etched portraits of ladies in the early literature. But in terms of the society in modern times, right down to the present, it's quite true to say that women play quite a dominant role.

BLACKBURN: Can we turn now to one of your best known poems, 'Coffins' [Cisteachan-laighe]? This is a darker poem, much more full of a sense of

157

hurt and loss than the first two we've spoken of.

The poem begins with memories of your grandfather and his joiner's workshop. A homely enough scene, it seems to me, and yet there are elements of hardness, even violence in it, with the mention of hammers and nails, saws and chisels.

THOMSON: And the thin, bare plank.

BLACKBURN: And immediately following this there is the remark about death, which was for the child you were then, something almost impossible to understand, like a glimmering of the darkness or a whisper of the stillness, both impossible, absurd things.

Well, after this, we move forward in time, to the event of your grandfather's own burial and even there death and coffins meant little to you. The little boy that was you only wanted home to 'talk, and tea, and warmth.'

THOMSON: Yes, that's it so far.

BLACKBURN: And then the poem moves from these memories of happenings in the school of life to memories of the actual school which you attended – and there were coffins there too. This time they were metaphorical coffins which were made by the joiners of the mind, the teachers. What they did was to take the natural, living, wood of your Gaelic self and turn it into coffins decorated with varnish and braid and brass, all things foreign to the wood itself, unnecessary additions. We have here, I think, the same sort of distinction as we've had in both of the previous poems, between things that are natural and essential, close to the heart of life, and things which don't matter all that much at all, and are out of place in your world.

So the conversion into coffins takes place

and the race is dying, but still you did not appreciate what was happening. It was not until you were grown up that the cold wind of Spring came bringing with it a realisation of what had happened and a sense of hurt and loss which was too great to be healed by anything like tea or talk, the comforts of home.

THOMSON: I think that the final reference to 'the cold wind of this Spring' would probably benefit from a little comment. This is an adult poem and a retrospective one, looking back on various stages of my own experience and lack of understanding. But the catalyst for this poem was in fact the publication of the Gaelic census figures for 1961, which appeared in 1963.

BLACKBURN: So the cold wind was for you the cold truth about the decline of Gaelic which was made evident by the census.

THOMSON: That's right. And it might be added that these intrusive influences which are referred to in the poem, the varnish and braid and so on begin by being somewhat external but in the course of time penetrate deeper and deeper. When I wrote the poem I was looking at the relatively external stage of the process. If I were to make a comment now, it would be much more positive and savage.

BLACKBURN: And the notion that the things like braid and brass will become more deeply part of the coffin, gives a very grim note indeed to the poem. We're talking now not only of pain and hurt but also of decay. This provides a very black undertone to the pathos at the end of the poem. Well, a lot of people admire this poem. I think it's a very good example of the type of poem which, although it is quite readily understood in a general sort of way at a first reading, grows and deepens as you look longer at it.

Well now, the poems we've looked at so far are drawn from your own memories of Lewis. But you write poems too of times in Lewis which were before your own. A poem which takes us back into the past is 'Strathnaver' ['Srath Nabhair'], a poem about the Clearances, when people were driven from their homes and from the lands they worked to make way for their landlord's sheep. Strathnaver, in Sutherland, was one of the areas most devastated by the Clearances. This, like 'Coffins', is a poem full of the sense of loss, even though there is a note of recovery and peace in the second part of it.

THOMSON: Strathnaver was cleared very completely and I suppose, in some ways very savagely.

BLACKBURN: In this poem you adopt a persona, that of the person whose father's house was burned. You recollect the burning and the star high up, far off from the event, which suggests to me a remoteness, an indifference almost on the part of heaven. Certainly the scene is set against a wide backcloth of eternity with the remote star winking down. And then the person of the poem goes on to remember that it was in the same year that the old woman was dragged out on to the dung heap. This, from what I remember reading, will be a reference to the occasion when an old woman, too weak to move herself, was lifted out of her house in a bed and placed on the dung heap while they, the factor's men, burned the house. Finally it is remarked how Strathnaver and the neighbouring Strath of Kildonan grow beautiful again, after these harrowing events, as the heather blooms again – like a woman who has suffered regaining her beauty only with an added depth and peace to it because of her suffering.

Now it's the bit in this poem about thatching the roof with snowflakes that Donald MacAulay once referred to as 'absurdist'.

THOMSON: Probably subconsciously it was because there are some situations where if you just come out with some sort of routine condemnation you are really underplaying the situation.

BLACKBURN: Yes, you feel the situation itself is so absurd, so outrageous, that you have to react to it in some crazy, flamboyant way. People do this, and not just in poetry either.

And then in the second verse there's the ironical bit about Scripture. The person imagines that the factors think that they are helping to fulfil a part of Biblical prophecy, though whether the estate factors thought at all about Scripture is very doubtful. The ministers of the time did though, and they often are said to have come out of the affair with little credit.

THOMSON: The Church at that time, it's fairly generally considered, took extraordinarily little interest in the plight of individuals and all too often just took the side of the evictors.

BLACKBURN: Saying to their flocks that what was happening to them was a punishment for their sins?

THOMSON: Oh yes. That point was often made.

BLACKBURN: So far we've considered poems which express in one way or another your accord, your sympathy, with your Gaelic tradition. But it's not all a rosy picture. There were elements in that past which you view with something less than enthusiasm, elements which are present still. I'm thinking particularly of those poems which express, or suggest, disapproval of some aspects of Calvinism, of the effects of Calvinism on the life of the people.

THOMSON: Throughout most of my life I've been critical

of certain aspects of the teaching, and of the character of the churches in the Highlands, and in the Islands especially. But I have been powerfully drawn to *some* features of the religious culture. There's no doubt at all in my mind that, at its best, that culture helps to mould a strong and thoughtful and caring character among people. I look back with the greatest of affection on some of the church people that I knew. But certainly some of the activity of the churches seemed to me to be totally destructive, and this was particularly true of the 'Free' churches – less so of the Church of Scotland. I'm thinking of their blanket condemnation of the local culture, the native culture, poetry and song and music and dance and all kinds of secular activities, most of which were perfectly harmless.

BLACKBURN: Yes. I think it's well to emphasise that Calvinism is not something which has always been part of the Highlands; it's a relatively latecomer. It came in its full force only in the course of the last century. It intruded into, superimposed itself upon, the older, native culture.

Well, how about looking at 'Scarecrow' ['Am bodach-ròcais']? It's about the coming of Calvin, Calvinism, to the Highlands and the Islands.

THOMSON: This is about the destructive force of Calvinism.

BLACKBURN: Can I again set my reading of it against what you make of it yourself? The scarecrow, the black-haired man wearing black clothes, is Calvin and he comes into the ceilidh-house, the place where people met to chat, to tell stories, to sing songs, to be sociable together. It was a place where people met at a sort of warm, human level; it was a physical centre for the community of people. Well, the black one comes and joins the company, with devastating effect: the cards fall from the hands of the players, the folktale freezes on the lips of the teller and something strange happens to the songs which the woman is singing – the goodness is taken out of their music.

THOMSON: I should perhaps say there that it was quite a commonly held belief that there were people, of the nature of witches, who could show their displeasure towards individuals by taking the goodness out of the milk, spoiling the cow's milk. So this is the analogy I had in mind.

BLACKBURN: Music and the milk; Calvin and the witch. Then we come to the point of change in the poem,

But he did not leave us empty handed:

The 'But' there is very strong. That's a feature of Gaelic writing, I think, the very forceful use of the word 'but' or 'nevertheless' to stop us in our tracks and give our thought a new, often more careful, direction. It's a feature I think of Gaelic talk, Gaelic thinking, not just of Gaelic writing, and maybe this is something that comes in a way from Calvinism. You've not to allow yourself to get carried away too enthusiastically by anything in the world; as soon as you do, up comes the 'but', the warning finger. Stop and consider.

THOMSON: (*Laughing*) Yes. Yes.

BLACKBURN: Well here the 'but' is strong, but it's really introducing an ironical statement because what Calvin puts into the hands of the people is not exactly what they might have chosen; they might have been better to be left empty-handed! Look what he gives.

163

THOMSON: He's giving the same sort of thing, songs, stories, but it's all foreign.

BLACKBURN: Yes, and there's a derogatory tone in the poem here, in the use of the words 'tales' and 'fragments': 'tales' sounds remote, not like stories which are somehow close to you, homely. And 'fragments' suggests things broken and incomplete and pretty worthless. And the songs will, I suppose, be psalms, sung in that very, very distinctive way of the Free churches – there's no sound like that I know of, not in this part of the world any-way. It's a sort of wailing from the bowels of the earth. To me, at its best, very moving, very sincere, very controlled, not hysterical. Well that I imagine, is the new song. And then there's the bit about the fire. But it is a cry from a fallen world. Not like the old songs at all. Now that's an important part, at the end of the poem. The fire in the ceilidh-house is a communal fire; it is in the centre of the people. (In fact it was often in the centre of the floor, with the smoke going out through a hole in the roof. It would be a peat fire.) Now Calvin sweeps this communal fire, this symbol of life and community (and fires of this sort are to be seen away back to the days of Druidic culture, Earth worship and the worship of Baal. Beltane, the festival of Spring has its name from the Gaelic Baal-teine, Baal-fire) . . . Calvin then sweeps this fire from the house and puts instead a hot fire in each individual and separate breast, the fire of Hell, the fear at least of Hell-fire. People are thus divided, each one fearful and preoccupied with his own concern to avoid such fire. Hell-fire and predestination are central things in Calvin's teaching.

THOMSON: Absolutely. Yes.

BLACKBURN: I don't think there's anything else I'd want to say about this poem, except to add that, again, it's one of those poems which grows under scrutiny. The more you look at it and the more you know of the culture, the more you see in it.

Before we leave this area of central concern in your work, Gaeldom and what has happened to it, can we have a moment with another small poem, 'When the dark comes' ['Nuair a thig an dorch']?

> When the dark comes
> over you, taking Muirneag away
> and Bayble Hill and Hòl,
> when your sheep are lying,
> the grass dark in the womb of night,
> the new moon not yet up,
> I shall throw this handful of peats on the fire
> and it will make some light.

BLACKBURN: This is the sort of poem which invites a reader to make his own meaning out of the images in it. What is symbolised by the dark, by the sheep, the womb of night and so on. What did you have in mind yourself when you wrote it?

THOMSON: I don't think there's any one explanation of it, not even from the writer's point of view. The predominant explanation in my case would be that the dark represents cultural loss, and the loss of a language and the possible death of a tradition. And the last line, about throwing some peats on the fire and making some light refers in part to the poems that I make which may illumine the scene for a little longer.

BLACKBURN: And the sheep are there, representing anything in your world that is cared for. The dark conveys a sense of desolation, and the mention of the new moon a sense of hope, a light to come. But in the meantime only the light of the handful of peats. And Muirneag and Bayble Hill and Hol are, of course, places dear to you which are lost in the darkness.

THOMSON: Yes. That's the way it works. And I agree entirely with you that there should be room for the reader to create his own poem in his mind; that's enormously important. It's one of the criteria of successful poems that ample room is left for variety of interpretation.

BLACKBURN: There's something, however, that perhaps should be said here. Although the poems at which we've been looking, do leave room for the reader to create his own experience from the text, there's not much doubt as to what the writer's attitudes are, what he likes and dislikes. I think this is one of the characteristics of Gaelic poetry. Feelings, attitudes, are made very explicit, very plain.

Maybe this has something to do with the past, the way the people had to live. I think difficult environments tend to make people direct and uncompromising in their attitudes.

THOMSON: Or it may have something to do with the particularly stark choices that Gaels find themselves confronted with at the present time, especially the Gaelic writer. These choices are often black and white ones and no doubt encourage the writers to take very positive and sometimes uncompromising attitudes. Once you find yourself in that position there is a distinct temptation to preach sermons about it. But I'm glad that you're drawing attention to the other aspects of the poetry that differentiate it from sermons.

BLACKBURN: Yes, the scope that's left for interpretation,

deliberately left. And, of course, the use that poetry makes of images, things one can see and feel and hear in the imagination. And the use of irony and rhythms and structure and so on. All these are among the elements of poetry.

THOMSON: And I would tend to stress too, what I see as one of the essential activities of many poets and that is the description of experience, the putting of whatever kind of experience it is into language. This relies heavily on the poet's power of observation, of detailed observation, and it's very characteristic of Gaelic poetry at all periods. There is the extremely elaborate kind of description which has its analogies in Celtic art, in manuscript illumination, in the intertwining lines of the Celtic cross and so on. And then obviously in the highest kind of description you need both close observation, and more importantly, sharp selection of what is significant. The more intellectual poets are able to make that selection more effectively than the less intellectual ones.

BLACKBURN: Yes, I've been thinking as you've been speaking that the descriptive tradition can be a very dangerous one if there's not a good mind at work, able to select well, and so able to avoid writing reams and reams of tedious detail which is not making any point or having any particular effect.

Now, as we come towards the end of our conversation, we should say that among your poems are some which reach out beyond Gaeldom, not just through the common appeal of what they have to say about the 'human condition', but in their subjects and their geographical locations too. I'm thinking of poems like 'Budapest' and 'Poem of Europe' and the poems about Glasgow, which are very bleak, some of them, like 'The Weight of the Stones' and the short one, 'Blood' ['Fuil'].

> Walking in the dusk here
> in the pock-marked streets,
> half-turned from the half-empty houses
> where people are watching TV,
> drawn by the light through the narrow
> windows,
> walking through the shadows
> through the storm that breaks
> on the aerials of the houses,
> through the disappointment
> and the broken promises
> on the smashed hearths,
> I saw blood on the wall.
>
> But I was afraid
> that it was not Christ's blood,
> nor the blood of the Jew defending
> Jerusalem,
> nor the blood of childbirth in new life's full
> flood.

BLACKBURN: So the blood at the end here is not in any way well spent; it is the blood of a violence that has been created by the surroundings and the disillusion you describe in the first part of the poem.

Another poem expressing disillusion, your own this time, is the neat little one, 'Rabbits' ['Rabaidean'].

THOMSON: Most of my life I've been interested in politics, particularly nationalist politics and this is a pretty disillusioned comment at the end of the 70s, at the time of the referendum about Scottish independence which failed, or was rigged or whatever. I was travelling a lot on the roads then, between Perthshire and Glasgow and this is how this one emerged.

A rabbit
in the car's headlight
almost safely
across the road
when it sensed danger,
when fear struck it.
It turned back.
You realise
there are sermons in rabbits
(Scottish ones)
this year.

BLACKBURN: A neat one.

However, I think we should finish with a poem which goes back to the subject of Lewis. It's a sad one in which it is realised that the picture you carry in your mind of the place, is better than the place itself as you find it on returning to it. So much that we care for is really in our mind, our dreams, rather than in the nature of things as we find them to be. But the dreams are important all the same: they keep us going, creating sometimes and hoping. Well – 'When I come back' ['Nuair a thilleas mi'] . . .

When I come back
the potato flowers will be out,
the bees humming,
the cows lowing to milking
when I come back.

When I arrive,
shaking you by the hand,
the coldness of the ring

will be on the palm of hope
when I arrive.

When I lie down
in your kind breast,
the cuckoo will come
and wailing with it,
when I lie down.

And when I rise
on that morning,
the ring will be shattered
and the cow dry
and the dark-brown island as I first knew it.

170

16. Iain Crichton Smith
(poems in English)
by
JOHN BLACKBURN

The dedicated spirits grow
in winters of pervasive snow
their crocus armour.
Their perpendiculars of light
flash sheerly through the polar night
with missionary fire.

from 'The Dedicated Spirits'

These lines form the first verse in the first collection of
Crichton Smith's poems, *The Long River*, published in
1955. They set the mood for what was to follow in the rest
of that fresh, penetrating and sometimes very lyrical early
collection. It is a mood which has continued throughout
his writing career. Always, in reading through his poetry,
or his short stories or one of his novels, one can be aware
of a dedicated spirit at work, probing, analysing, attempt-
ing to understand. Writing, for Crichton Smith, is not a
pastime: it involves a serious engagement with the lives
of people. 'Poetry,' he once said, 'should not be a game.
. . . Poetry is not an affair of words. People have to feel
what you are talking about is meaningful and important
to them. And if it isn't, then it's a failure. I always come
back to that.'

Since the main preoccupations to be found in Crichton
Smith's poetry have their origins in his early, and in some

171

ways exceptional, experience on the Isle of Lewis, where he was reared in the same village as Derick Thomson, it seems best to begin this consideration of his poetry by referring to some of the most distinctive features of that experience.

Bare Lewis Iain Crichton Smith was born in Glasgow in 1928, but when he was very young he was taken to Lewis, 'bare Lewis without tree or branch', where he was brought up by his widowed mother in the crofting township of Bayble. Life was hard there among the elements of wind and moor, sea and rock.

'There were ghosts at the edge of the dyke and heather on Hol, and the stone round it. And an owl in the wave, and a wind shaking Mary Roderick, and the hen being blown to the moor. At the tips of our fingers was the dream. But the wind took low Bayble away. The boats are coming towards uncultivated soil. . . .
   What is that cloud on the Muirneag? What is that Bible opening and the leaves with the wind and the rain on them?'

The wind seems to dominate everything in these lines, drowning the owl, blowing the hen to the open moor, taking Bayble itself away and bringing storm and rain to the opening Bible. Elsewhere 'winds/howl from the vacant north' and we find an image, part-borrowed from an earlier Gaelic poet, of

a blind man hunting a key
on a night of terror and storm.

The isle is indeed full of strange noises, but they all speak, in such lines, of barrenness and coldness and darkness. There was beauty too: 'I remember a frosty night and the world open, south to north. O the sparkling sea was my choice.' and 'the ripening moon of the barley, the golden moon of the long night, the moon of the boys, the moon of Lewis . . .' Sparkling, ripening, golden . . . there is colour here and a sense of vitality and fulfilment. But it is the darker, harsher elements which predominate in the recorded memories of Lewis.

Besides the harshness of the natural environment Crichton Smith remembers too the harshness of living in a home where there was very little money.

> Our life wasn't really very rich in any way; we were really very poor. We were brought up, three of us, I've got two brothers, on a pension of about 18/- a week . . . Actually, we used to have salt herring and potatoes every day of the week except Sunday. On Sunday, for some strange religious reason, we had meat and soup. But Monday, Tuesday, Wednesday, Thursday, Friday and Saturday we used to have potatoes and herring.

Another hard, pervasive, aspect of life on Lewis which bore in upon Crichton Smith's mind was the amount of dying that took place around him. He remembers the bright, yellow-ringed eyes of the hens in the creels, waiting to be killed; he would see the hordes of fish being landed, the dead sheep on the hills; he knew, of course, that his father had died and he knew, too, a young friend dying of tuberculosis, a common disease in the islands up till recent times. And he knew well about the terrible disaster which occurred when the steamship *Iolaire* struck the Rocks of Holm, at the entrance to Stornoway Harbour on New Years Eve in 1918 and sank with the loss of nearly two hundred men of the island – soldiers and sailors returning home to Lewis after the end of World War I. Their bodies were washed ashore on New Year's Day. He tells of another occasion when one of his uncles, shipwrecked, was heard singing songs in the darkness while clinging to a rock, hoping it seems, to guide the rescuers to him. When they reached the rock there was no one on it.

Crichton Smith's memories of his island then are not like Edwin Muir's memories of his Orcadian childhood, full of sunshine and security. Life on Lewis as remembered by Crichton Smith, though not without its sunshine, was full of darker, sterner elements. There was, moreover, among these one, not yet mentioned, which has been of particular significance in the life and poetry of Crichton Smith – Calvinism. It is virtually impossible, I think, to appreciate, or even to understand properly, much of the poetry of Crichton Smith without some notion of the nature of Calvinism and of the people who believe in its doctrines.

Calvinism, it is well to observe in passing, is not a form of Christianity which has always been dominant in the Highlands and Islands. It came into its full vigour only in the nineteenth century, and it was by no means welcomed by everyone. Some areas remained firmly Roman Catholic while others adopted or included less stringent forms of Protestantism. (Derick Thomson's poem 'The Scarecrow' makes sharp comment upon the coming of Calvinism to the Highlands.)

To the Calvinist, life is not something infinitely precious beyond which lies oblivion. Nor is it, for that matter, an existence for the spirit to pass through while it reaches out in ritual, or in music, poetry, art or love to a great spirit and an afterlife beyond present experience. We are, the Calvinist believes, born into life in a state of original sin, damned by Eve's wickedness and Adam's complicity in the Garden of Eden. When we die, we leave life for eternal damnation, unless we are of the elect, one of those chosen by God for acceptance into Heaven. There is nothing we can do which will alter our fate in this matter: that is predestined, pre-ordained by an all-knowing God from the beginning of time. To have any hope of salvation we must believe in Christ as our Saviour, and we must obey God's laws. It is prudent, (though in view of predestination perhaps not logical) to do so, for then we lay ourselves open to the inner awareness, the call from God, that will tell us that we are among those redeemed by the blood of Christ, saved from the fires of Hell.

Now for those who believe in such a vision of life and death, the things of this life are of little significance compared to the state of one's being in the life to come. The beauty of nature, for instance, is only a kind of decoration on a fallen world; the arts of man are unimportant – what can they reveal to us of anything that really matters? The joys and passions of man are things of tainted flesh and blood and his casual entertainments are trivial fillers of time. Indeed, all such things as these are seen as potential dangers, as they may lead the minds of those who engage in them away from belief and prayer and obedience and listening for the call from God.

Crichton Smith recalls how his mother and her friends, women of the island, would refer to some ministers as 'wooden ministers', meaning that these men did not have the power in their preaching to excite and terrify their congregations with the threat of Hell-fire. Ministers were expected to rouse their congregations to fear and tremble. He recalls, too, how once his mother found him making little wooden hens in the shed beside the house. She asked him, 'Why do you make wooden hens when the Lord has made real ones?' Why, in other words, do you waste your time doing something that is unnecessary and quite pointless? Better to gather eggs, which the Lord has supplied for us, or to read your Bible.

It is out of this background then, that there came one of Crichton Smith's early poems, 'Poem of Lewis', in which the people's disregard for poetry becomes, by the end of the poem, a disregard for the 'great forgiving spirit of the word', the word that is, not only of poetry, but of God's mercy, spoken of in the Bible and symbolised in the heavens by the rainbow.

Poem of Lewis

Here they have no time for the fine graces
of poetry, unless it freely grows
in deep compulsion, like water in the well,

175

woven into the texture of the soil
in a strong pattern. They have no rhymes
to tailor the material of thought
and snap the thread quickly on the tooth.
One would have thought that this black north
was used to lightning, crossing the sky like fish
swift in their element. One would have thought
the barren rock would give a value to
the bursting flower. The two extremes,
mourning and gaiety, meet like north and south
in the one breast, milked by knuckled time,
till dryness spreads across each aging bone.
They have no place for the fine graces
of poetry. The great forgiving spirit of the word
fanning its rainbow wing, like a shot bird
falls from the windy sky. The sea heaves
in visionless anger over the cramped graves
and the early daffodil, purer than a soul, is gathered
   into the terrible mouth of the gale.

The Voyage Out

About us the horizon bends
its orphan images, and winds
howl from the vacant north.
The mapless navigator goes
in search of the unscented rose
he grows in his heart's south.
   (from 'The Dedicated Spirits')

It must be no surprise if out of 'this black north' a sensitive and intelligent young man might wish to go in search of whatever roses the south might bloom for him, and in search, too, of an environment where his mind might observe and come to terms with the world in its own way, free of the bounds imposed upon it by Calvinist teaching. What I want to consider now are some of the poems which mark stages in the voyage out.

'Some Days Were Running Legs' is an interesting poem from *The Long River*. The first two of the unrhymed quatrains are full of images of light and happiness. The writer remembers days in his boyhood, days which were full of the running legs of children at play, glowing sunsets and the old men of the township promising that the next day would be a fine one too (Red sky at night, the shepherd's delight. . .). He remembers nights, evenings, when he parted from his companions as they all went home and he remembers that they wished for nothing more than that a new day should come for them to play in, throwing stones at sticks in the water, or perhaps, at telegraph poles.

Then in verse three comes a change: the images become harsher, darker, more violent. We have seen the joy and the sunlight; now we are meeting with the other side of experience in Lewis. The rain, destructively, floods forever the green pasture and the horses turn their backs to the wind, so indicating the approach of a storm. At the coast, the rocks which rise out of the sea are grey, colourless, and sharp. And the sea itself is referred to as ancient, so that one thinks of it as being dull and grey around the rocks. The violence and the darkness in the imagery here are matched by a roughening of the sound of the poem: after the incontinent f sounds in the rain flooding forever, there come the firm, hard sounds of the bs and ts before the final harshness of the letter r as the rocks rise into the poem.

The violence in the imagery is continued into the fourth and last verse, where reference is made to the custom of covering mirrors with shawls or blankets, for fear the lightning should strike at them. It is possible that the shine of the mirror was thought likely to attract the lightning, but a more probable explanation for this being done is that the mirror would be seen as a sign of earthly vanity and so as something which should be covered when God's wrath was rolling round the heavens. It was not a fear so much of tempting lightning as of tempting God. The sense of violence and threat here is increased by the

177

mention of the eel and its speed. The lightning comes out of the sky, its element, with the speed of the flashing eel of the deeps. The island is caught between the violence of sky and sea, surrounded by darkness and flashing light.

Then come the last two lines. where calm returns, though still there remain the two, contrasting, aspects of light and dark, violence and gentleness. The black crows come squawking through the evening sky in the broken, flapping, second last line,

'Black/ the roman rooks/ came/ from the left/ squawking' before the evening in the last line flows gently back around their wings. The word 'evening' with its long first syllable lengthens the sound of the line – 'It's a very mellifluous line' was Crichton Smith's own comment on it. Perhaps then, at the end of the poem, peace and gentleness have the last word, but the poem is essentially one of contrasts; the conflicting aspects of life on Lewis are set against each other in what Crichton Smith likes to call 'a war of opposites', a sort of inner dialectic.

(It is perhaps worth pointing out in passing that this 'war of opposites' is reflected in the titles of Crichton Smith's books of this early period: and *Thistles and Roses*, *The Law and The Grace*, *The Black and the Red* – a collection of short stories.)

The last lines of 'Some Days' require a little further comment. Why roman rooks (with a small r at roman!) and why mention that they come from the left? The left is easily explained. The left hand, to the Romans, was sinister, the one which held the dagger, hidden, while the right hand was outstretched in greeting. So, left/sinister, Romans, violence – it all suits the mood of the poem towards its end. But still, why Romans at all?

The connection in Crichtons Smith's mind was between the black flapping wings of the violent crows and the black flapping gowns, togas, of the Romans, themselves men of violence and heavy authority. But, the reader objects, 'the Romans did not wear black gowns at all; their togas were white!' Precisely, but to Crichton Smith, reared under the black gowns of the ministers and teachers of Lewis, all gowns worn by violent authority were thought of as black. He did not recollect the whiteness that belonged to other worlds beyond Lewis. Crows, clergy, dominies, romans, blackness, all come together in the poet's mind, the Romanness of the Romans being reduced by a small r, not to disrupt the poem too much with a foreign image.

Not perhaps the happiest moment in Crichton Smith's poetry, in terms of fact and precision, but a moment that gives us a very clear impression of the force of his feeling about the darker side of his experience in Lewis.

When Crichton Smith wrote 'Some Days' he was not conscious of writing a poem which was expressive of the dichotomy, the 'war of opposites' in his mind about Lewis. He was, he thought, simply jotting down memories. Poets are not always aware of what is moving within them: sometimes it is not until years after writing that they perceive the ground swell that carried the poems to the surface.

When he wrote 'Old Woman', however, he was fully aware of what he was doing, creating a picture of a woman of whom he disapproved, a woman steeped in the blackness of the crows and the black gowns. Some have felt in this poem a certain sense of sympathy for the woman; but Crichton Smith himself did not feel such or intend to convey such. 'I had no sympathy for this woman at all . . . She is all law and no grace.'

In the first part of the poem, the black life of the woman is pictured. She has to labour under the creel full of peats, feeling its thorns in her back. She has no regard for the beauty of the daffodils (Consider the lilies – or the daffodils – of the field how they grow . . .). She steadily stamps upon them. She wishes all wrongdoers to be punished for their wickedness. Even God, she believes, has no right to grant them mercy. She watches, with cold eyes, as her husband comes home drunk from the public bar, which in her mind is as bad as Sodom, that city of evil among men. Her baby in the cradle is to her a sinful thing, conceived in the fleshly act of union and born a creature with the original sin of Adam and Eve within it. Round her children, as they grow, she builds stone walls – perhaps literally, certainly metaphorically. Then, before the final statements about her 'present' condition, there comes the verse directing attention to herself, not to what she did but to what she was. Her hair (her head? her mind? her life?) was enclosed in a scarf of grey, imprisoned, it seems, by her cultural inheritance. Yet in that scarf, the hair burns yellow and is likened to the wildly falling mountain spray. Here we have a suggestion of life and vitality: her hair is linked to the daffodil by its colour. Yet the hair does not seem altogether healthy: it is burning only slowly.

Her life, her liveliness, enclosed by a grey culture and thorns in her back. There is a case here, perhaps, for sympathy. But Crichton Smith does not make it. He presses on relentlessly picturing the wrongness of her life, the life to which she submitted and through which she harmed the lives of others. He shows her alone among the brass that always demands to be polished, again and again, reflecting, as it were, her *own* relentlessness. Around her too are the slow silences of old age and the sinful mirrors which she will look in with a sense of guilt. (The glass could refer to the whisky glasses of her husband which would not be destroyed but kept frugally and with a sense of respect for the dead. These however, are more likely to be in a cupboard, out of sight.) Alone then she lives in her room, she who, never even with all the experience life could offer her, learned to forgive ordinary, common humanity on its way to the grave.

Outside, in contrast, life flourishes. The deer, associated in Crichton Smith's writing with passion and pride and swiftness, look down from their hills, the daffodils wave in the breezes in the valleys and the huge sea sings over the headland and the cry of the peevish crow, the black symbol of herself. (In Gaelic reference is often made to the music of the sea – ceol na mara.)

The similarities between this old woman and the old

woman, Mrs Scott, in Crichton Smith's best known prose work, *Consider the Lilies*, are obvious. Mrs Scott is no heroine. She, too, is black and crowlike until in the latter stages of the novel we see her learning in the house of MacLeod to feel something of the beauty and love to be had in life.

Old women appear often in the writings of Crichton Smith. I think his interest in the old woman is to be accounted for, partly, by the fact that for many years he was closely associated with his mother, looking after her in her old age. The figure of the old woman, however, is common not only in Crichton Smith's work; it is common throughout Gaelic literature. Indeed, the figure of the old, or mature woman, the mother figure, is prominent both in literature and in society wherever Celtic culture is found. It is interesting, for example, to notice how many old or mature women are given positions of central importance in the writings of twentieth-century Irishmen – Shaw, O'Casey, Synge, Yeats – and Yeats referred to Ireland itself as 'the old woman'. So, Crichton Smith is not alone in his fascination for this almost archetypal figure. The figure goes, in fact, far back into Celtic mythology where 'na cailleach' presided over that part of the year from the end of Autumn to the coming of Spring. She was the Winter Hag, the old woman of coldness and darkness, who brought with her a reminder of our mortality.

When the reign of the cailleach was over her place was taken, in May, by the Bridu, the Spring Maiden, who ruled from then until Sabhain, the Festival of the Dead at the end of October. In the poem 'Two Girls Singing' we find ourselves in the company of two echoes of that Spring Maiden, singing their way through a late November night. Memories of bare Lewis and disapproval of those whose lives are devoted only to the Law of the Bible and the necessities of living are put aside here. Instead, it is the human sweetness of the singing which captures the attention. We have met with what Crichton Smith calls 'one of these unpredictable moments of

181

grace'.

There was a time when he travelled regularly from Oban to Dumbarton, near Glasgow, to visit his mother who lived alone there. The journey was made in a cold bus, full of pale yellow light, which pitched and lurched on lochside roads and down glens through the winter nights, for hours on end. It was an unpleasant, sometimes nauseating experience. Crichton Smith remembers:

> 'One night I was on the bus. It was a very dreary
> journey and it was very cold and it was very dark.
> Then suddenly, at the back of the bus, two girls
> started singing a song. It was sort of unpredictable:
> I hadn't expected that anyone would sing on that
> bus – and, it was so moving, and human . . . And
> this yellow. I always associate yellow with the
> yellow street lights in cities, these harsh yellow
> street lights shining down on the streets. The
> yellow to me seems to be something mechanical
> and hostile – and then there was the harmony of
> these girls and the fact that suddenly out of the
> bus, for no reason at all, almost like birds . . . it
> doesn't matter what they were singing. It was just
> the singing, the fact that they were singing in that
> bus . . . the unpredicted voices of our kind.'

So, we have come in this poem a fair distance from the Lewis of his memories. The same might be said when looking at 'Jean Brodie's Children'. In that poem it is the Edinburgh of 'winter cakes and tea' which is remembered, the Edinburgh where days are 'all green and shady' and schoolmistresses 'iron in their certainty' though inwardly 'trembling on grey boughs'. Here we are among the grace notes of Crichton Smith's poetry. Such notes, it may be observed, are none too common in the work of this writer who, although among the most hilarious of companions, is in his poetry nearly always intensely serious. And this thought brings us to the next stage in our consideration, the matter of his Lewis in-

heritance, what he brought with him from the bare
island.

The Inheritance   It would be wrong to think of Crichton
Smith as having brought nothing from his experience
in Lewis but a desire to seek for moments of colour and
human warmth and sweetness. He took also with him
from his island home other, sterner, preoccupations. Although Crichton Smith is not at one with Calvin as to the
existence and nature of God and Heaven and Hell and
damnation, he has inherited the Calvinistic cast of
mind which obliges one to search out the truth of things,
in particular the truth about evil and guilt and suffering.
One must, he believes, face the nature of the world and
the nature of people and the nature of oneself, as they
really are and one must not allow any lies or pretences
or comforting make-believe or decoration to obscure
matters.

In 'Love Songs of a Puritan', this fierce dedication to
truth is to be seen in the view which he takes of the poet's
function, of his own function at least. It is the poet's task
to stand steady and to record what he sees, no matter
how terrible it is. This he must do without becoming involved in abstract language, large 'conceptual' words
which are empty of feeling, and perhaps of meaning too.
The poet has to stay close to 'the living grass', the actual
things of life, the sights, sounds, scents and inner trem-
blings that make up the world of man. These he must
perceive and feel and truly record, good or ill as they may
be.

In 'John Knox' something of this dedication is seen in
the gusto which the poet displays in his approval of
Knox's attack on the *false* French roses of Mary Queen
of Scots. It is not beauty which Knox attacks in this poem
but idleness and affectation, which is a kind of lie.

The shearing naked absolute blade has torn
through false French roses to her foreign cry.

Here we find a disgusted, dismissive tone created by the

alliterated fs. It is, as Crichton Smith once remarked, a very sexy poem. There was more, he imagined, to Knox's own feelings about Mary and her ladies than just a puritan's disapproval of their ways.

In 'Face of an Old Highland Woman', we find 'the art and dance of Europe', all that huge culture, being presented as something almost trivial in comparison to the fundamental power of the peasant face of the old woman which is likened to the earth itself, the very landscape from which it emerges.

Even stronger expressions of this puritan inheritance, this urgent pursuit of the truth however unpleasant, are to be found in Crichton Smith's Gaelic poems, especially those in *Biobuill is Sanasan Reice (Bibles and Advertisements)*, 1965, translations of which are to be found in *The Permanent Island*, 1975. In, for instance, the short poem 'At the Stones of Callanish' human barbarity is seen as enduring through the centuries, from the fires of the druids to the fires of nuclear warfare

At the stones of Callanish yesterday I heard one
woman saying to another: 'This is where they
burnt the children in early times.' I did not see the
druids among the planets nor sun nor robe: but I
saw a beautiful blue ball like heaven cracking and
children with skin hanging to them like the flag in
which Nagasaki was sacrificed.

This puritanical drive for truth and for fundamental values is one of the major features of Crichton Smith's writing which seems to have its roots in his early experience on Lewis. There is, however, another major, and gentler, theme in his work which also seems to derive from his upbringing on the island and that is the theme of community. Living as part of a community, a relatively small community, and caring for others within it is something which goes far back into the history of the Gael. Kinship and clan were very important to the 'loch-divided' Gael living among the mountains and moorlands and glens of the Highlands. Moreover, Calvinism, through its insistence on Bible study and the observance of the laws of God, seems to have reinforced the tradition of community. Man is called upon to have care for his neighbour.

The importance of community and the dangers inherent in living in isolation from others are highlighted time and again in Crichton Smith's writing. The old woman in 'Old Woman' is isolated in her own bitter, black world. Mrs Scott in *Consider the Lilies* is isolated; the school-teacher in *The Blot*, an excellent short story, is isolated, loveless – and the old woman in her pupil's story peers through her letter box, waiting for the postman to bring her some contact with the world outside. In a different way, the policeman in *Jimmy and the Policeman* is isolated: he mixes with the people of the community all the time in his daily round and yet is apart from them because he is officious, law-minding, instead of people-minding. Then again, in one of his best known short stories, 'The Hermit', one sees the devastating effects which the presence of a hermit, who lives on the outskirts of the community and sometimes passes through it, has on the lives of the people. The village is disintegrating until the schoolmaster, who sees the danger, resorts to a low and unfair trick to oblige the hermit to leave.

This kind of isolation, the isolation of those who live apart from others is the predominant one in Crichton Smith's work. But there is another which has troubled him from the early days of his writing and that is the isolation of the mind from the world which lies beyond it. How can we know what other people really think or why they think it? How can we know the world of the deer, or the seagull?

There is nothing anyone can do with these
sheer naked wills that dominate this sea.
Nearer to stone
than to a thinking man
they have no cruel look or kind. Amuse

yourself with fantasies, these will not come
out of the different air which is their home.

How can we use language to link us to the world out
there, beyond us? Are we not perhaps creating in our languages our own worlds for ourselves as we go, thinking
that what we say applies quite simply to the world
around us?

It is against this background then, that we can see why
he approves in 'A Young Highland Girl Studying Poetry'
of the fact that the girl does not need the comfort of poetry, or of philosophy for that matter: she can find her
happiness elsewhere for she belongs to a tradition, a community, a way of life which is good. Her kind, her ancestors, were not crushed by the hardships of their lives
which were lived close to the earth, their lambs, their
children. The 'foreign rose' of Calvinism did not make
them mournful for they were at one with the ways of the
older culture with its dancing and its fears of the stars
and the seas. These people believed in the curative powers of waters: they were pagan and mystical, fond of children and of love and *they* needed neither poetry nor the
preachings of solemn ministers (abstractions of the grave)
about death and the hereafter. He, on the other hand, the
poet, the natural flyer, alone in his skies finds a certain
bitter satisfaction in his art and in his insights but still he
recognises that she, like her people before her, has other
rewards of a more earthbound kind. She, he concludes,
will know a husband as he makes his journey with her
through life to the grave, blessing her on the way by
many acts of love. (In bygone days, in Elizabethan times
for example, the act of sexual union was known as 'a little
death' – hence the concluding line 'but he by many
deaths will bless her days.')

'A Young Highland Girl Studying Poetry' is a highly
allusive poem, that is one which depends for its full effects on the reader knowing about the matters to which
it refers. But it is, I think, a very full and beautiful poem
written in admiration of a way of life which Crichton

Smith saw continuing in the being of the young girl in his classroom, a girl cut off no doubt from the intense experience which contact with poetry and the other 'high' arts can give, but likely to be at peace in her own world with herself and her community.

Praise Poetry   Praise poetry has a long tradition in Gaelic poetry, right back to the time of the bards. Crichton Smith's praise poetry, unlike that of the bards, is not lavish and hyperbolic: it is restrained, thoughtful, and it is often addressed, as one might expect, not to heroes, but to quiet, 'ordinary' people of his own acquaintance. 'For Angus MacLeod' and 'For My Mother' are two such poems which are in the *Gallery* selection. In each the lines which close the poem are perhaps the most memorable, expressing as they do the lonely, stoical quality of the people he admires. In 'For My Mother', he pictures his mother, when she was only seventeen, standing at dawn, a herring girl, on 'a hard Lowestoft quay':

the lonely figure in the doubtful light
with the bloody knife beside the murmuring sea
waiting for the morning to come right.

In 'For Angus MacLeod', he ends with a fine compliment to MacLeod for the influence which he had upon his pupils:

His best editions are some men and women
who scrutinise each action like a word.
The truest work is learning to be human
definitive texts the poorest can afford.

There is praise, too, for great ones, men who committed themselves to thinking deeply and dangerously, who set out on 'the long river' of thought knowing that they might never reach secure land again. Freud's massive contribution to the understanding of the mind, for example, is viewed with deep respect, and apprehension,

187

> Great man from Vienna who opened the mind with a
> knife . . .

The Freud poems are translations from the Gaelic as is
also 'You Are at the Bottom of My Mind', which Crichton
Smith describes as 'a post-Freud love poem'. It is about
one whose nature he cannot understand yet whose memory haunts the deep recesses of his mind, as the image
of the diver with his helmet and his two great eyes
haunts the bottom of the sea.

> You went astray among the mysterious foliage of the
>   sea-bottom in the
> green half-light without love.
> And you will never rise to the surface of the sea, even
>   though my hands
> should be ceaselessly hauling, and I do not know your
>   way at all, you
> in the half-light of your sleep, haunting the bottom of
>   the sea without
> ceasing, and I hauling and hauling on the surface of
>   the ocean.

So, still here the search for beauty and for truly knowing, and still the sense of isolation. Our navigator is not
mapless now, as he claimed to be at the start of the long
river, but he is still hauling and hauling on the surface
of the ocean, still in a state of quest – and that I suppose
is the fate, and fortune, of any such committed writer. It
is worth mentioning that his latest volume of verse is
called *The Exiles*.

17. Seamus Heaney
by
GEDDES THOMSON

There's something faintly disturbing about taking some of Seamus Heaney's poems and putting them in a book away from the others. He is a poet to explore and enjoy as a whole. In his work you will find a world which is easy and difficult; where childhood memories, family life, humour, friendship and history interact much as they do in everyone's everyday life.

Seamus Heaney was born at Mossbawn in County Derry, Northern Ireland, in 1939. His father was a Catholic farmer. Heaney was 'the clever one' of a large family. He won a scholarship from the local primary school (which was 'mixed' in religion) to St Columb's College, a Catholic boarding-school for boys in Londonderry. From there he went on to Queen's University in Belfast where he gained a first-class honours degree in English. After a decade's teaching in Belfast he moved south to the Irish Republic in 1971, where he has lived ever since.

This potted biography of Heaney resonates with significance for his work as a poet, because his poetry is strongly autobiographical; not in the sense that he is narrowly confined to his own experience, but rather that he uses his own experience as a firm base from which to explore the world.

For example, Heaney's rural background provides a starting-point for almost all his poetry, but especially his early work, which is often an exploration of the meaning of childhood experiences on his father's farm. Although he has left the land (the first of his family to do so) for educational and literary success in the wider world, he returns to it again and again – not as an obsession, not for sentimental reasons – but to come to terms with Ireland's troubled history.

'Digging' was the first poem in Heaney's first collection. As such it conveniently illustrates some of his central concerns and stands as a statement of his central aim – as his ancestors dug with spades, so he will 'dig' with his pen. Digging, in fact, is a central, crucial image for Heaney. In his later poetry he reveals a fascination with archaeological history, in particular for the victims of ancient ritual killings perfectly preserved deep in the bogland his ancestors worked for a living, killings which provide a telling link with the violent present.

'Digging' itself integrates past and present very effectively. Notice how, in the middle of the second verse, childhood memories spring up with a vivid, almost painful reality – his father digging potatoes 'twenty years away'. The language is mouth-filling, but exact. Sound does not overcome sense.

> The coarse boot nestled on the lug, the shaft
> Against the inside knee was levered firmly

Heaney has always admired the expertise and rhythm of rural manual work; the tasks his ancestors performed for generations. Thus we have poems about ploughmen, blacksmiths, thatchers, potato gatherers or, as here, his father digging potatoes, which leads him further back to the heroic figure of his grandfather who could

> cut more turf in a day
> Than any other man on Toner's bog

The poem is built, like so much of Heaney's work, on verbs, particularly present participles and precise adverbial phrasing:- 'rasping', 'straining', 'stooping', 'levered firmly', 'corked sloppily' 'nicking and slicing neatly'. The most important verb, of course, is 'digging' (and its variants) which occurs three times in important positions towards the ends of stanzas.

The switch back to the present in the last two stanzas, the sudden change from the physical to the psychological in 'living roots awaken in my head', is typical of Heaney. Suddenly the poem is deepened in a most satisfying way, to make us read again and think. And when we do read it again, listening to its sensible music, we are struck by its ambivalence. The pen is powerful, 'snug as a gun', and Heaney will 'dig with it', but it is also 'squat' which suggests an ugliness and lack of rhythm to contrast with the easy expertise of manual labour. He has laid down his ancestors' spade to take up the pen but he does it, not boastfully, but with a sense of inadequacy, a twinge of guilt:

I've no spade to follow men like them.

The 'reverse' or contrast in the final stanza is a frequent structure in Heaney's early work. An experience is explored until a deepening or contrasting conclusion is reached. In 'Death of a Naturalist' the frogs, passive objects of school nature study and childhood games in the first stanza, become the terrifying 'slime kings' of the final stanza. In 'Follower' time inevitably reverses the father-son situation:

But today
It is my father who keeps stumbling
Behind me, and will not go away.

'Shore Woman', a later poem, has a much more complex structure. Indeed, it is a very subtle poem. In it Heaney adopts the persona of a fisherman's wife who tells us of a profoundly disturbing experience when she was helping her husband to fish for mackerel. This poem has no neat reversal because it is built on contrasts *and* ambiguities – the man's greedy and business-like approach to the task as opposed to the woman's intuitive realisation that 'this is so easy that it's hardly right' the terror and mystery of the sea as opposed to the 'safety' of the shore.

And what is the poem, finally, 'about'? There are more than hints that the woman is unhappy with her husband, that he 'puts her through it' in every sense. She has 'to get away from him' and his uncouth habits, but she can only escape to a 'fallow avenue', which perhaps suggests a loveless and childless marriage.

But how dangerous it would be to reduce all the events and elements in the poem to neat symbols. That would be to fall into the same business-like prosaic error as the husband who is foolishly determined to put their lives in danger to rebut what he considers a 'yarn'.

The poem is prefaced by a Gaelic proverb, 'Man to the hills, woman to the shore', but the woman's experience (and we sympathise with *her* point of view) while it confirms this glib aphorism in one sense, totally contradicts it in another. Life is more difficult and mysterious than its easy, glib surface. The woman realises this, but her husband never will. We are supposed to realise it as well.

'Docker' brings us to another unignorable aspect of Heaney's life and work – he is a Northern Irish Catholic. Like all public figures in Northern Ireland he has been under pressure to take a 'stand' on the issues raised by the violent sectarianism of his native province. He has been criticised, for example, for not condemning outright the activities of the IRA and from the other side, for not seeming committed enough to the Republican cause. His move to the south in 1971 was seen in some quarters as a 'cop-out', an attempt to escape the pressures attendant on being a famous Catholic poet in divided Belfast.

In fact, Heaney does *not* evade the Northern Ireland situation in his poetry. 'Docker' is particularly significant in this respect because it was written in the early 1960's *before* the present troubles and Heaney shows an artist's prophetic inkling of what was to come in the lines:

> That fist would drop a hammer on a Catholic –
> Oh yes, that kind of thing could start again

The poem is a portrait of a Protestant shipyard worker, probably an employee of Harland and Wolff's the giant Belfast yard, which has traditionally been a place where 'no Catholics need apply'. As so very often, Heaney uses the terms of a trade, transforms them into images to define the man:–

> The cap juts like a gantry's crossbeam,
> Cowling plated forehead and sledgehead jaw.
> Speech is clamped in the lips' vice

It is a portrait of a strong, silent, intensely narrow individual, conditioned by everything in his environment to keep down Catholicism. But is it just a portrait of a bigot? There is a perhaps surprising image in the final verse:

> He sits strong and blunt as a Celtic cross

Does that suggest that he and his like are just as much a part of the traditional landscape as any Irish Catholic, that, like Heaney's father in 'Follower', he 'will not go away'? To some Republicans this would seem a weak and needless concession, but I think it provides a clue to Heaney's attitude. Like any artist he seeks to understand, to dig for poetic truth rather than political dogma.

'Strange Fruit' and 'Casualty' provide further illustrations of Heaney's approach to the tragic reality of violence. Both poems concern the victims of ritual killings; the first from Europe's distant Iron Age past and the second from Northern Ireland's present. Heaney has indicated in prose and verse, that he sees a connection between the two.

'Strange Fruit' is one of a group of poems about the perfectly preserved bodies of Iron Age victims of ritual killings which were discovered in marsh-land in Denmark. Others are 'The Tollund Man', 'Punishment' and 'The Grauballe Man'. The poems are characterised by the poet's emotions of horror, fascination and deep pity for the victims. The girl in 'Strange Fruit', 'outstaring what had begun to feel like reverence', is described in terms which reveal these conflicting reactions. She is beautiful, delicate, fascinating, an object of awe and reverence from our archaeological heritage, but above all she is dead, a victim. Hence the ambiguity of phrases such as 'the wet fern of her hair', 'leathery beauty', 'perishable treasure', leading to the hammer-blows of:

Murdered, forgotten, nameless, terrible.

In other poems Heaney makes clearer the connection he sees between the murdered forgotten victims of long ago and what is happening in Northern Ireland today. For example, in 'The Grauballe Man' he writes of the 'hooded victim,/slashed and dumped' and suddenly we are made to think of the murderous contemporary activities of terrorist organisations on both sides of Ulster's sectarian divide.

'Punishment' is even more explicit. A girl has been hanged, her body dumped into the ancient marshland, as punishment for her adultery, and Heaney is irresistibly reminded of the Catholic girls who have been shaved, tarred and feathered by the IRA for going with British soldiers. The two important verses which refer to these girls reveal how Heaney is divided between pity for the victims and understanding of the reasons for the barbaric punishment –

I who have stood dumb
when your betraying sisters,
cauled in tar,
wept by the railings,

who would connive
in civilized outrage
yet understand the exact
and tribal, intimate revenge

'Casualty', which is about a friend of Heaney's who was murdered for breaking an IRA curfew imposed after Bloody Sunday in Londonderry, contains lines which almost exactly echo those in 'Punishment':

How culpable was he
That last night when he broke
Our tribe's complicity?

Notice the ambiguity in these quotations. Heaney writes in the first person plural of 'our tribe', admitting, even stating, that he is of the Catholic and Republican persuasion. He 'understands' the 'tribal revenge'. But notice again the words 'connive' and 'complicity' which suggest his deep unease in the face of such merciless violence.

'Casualty', is one of my own favourite Heaney poems. It is a tribute to the type of skilful country craftsman whom the poet has always admired and I find in it a powerful personal note of sadness for the fisherman friend who just had to disobey the edict of the IRA, not out of political disagreement or selfish indifference, but because –

he drank like a fish
Nightly, naturally
Swimming towards the lure
Of warm lit-up places,
The blurred mesh and murmur
Drifting among glasses
In the gregarious smoke.

Savour the music and quiet rhythms first of all, before you gradually unroll the 'swaddling band' of this poem's meaning. When you come to examine the imagery you will find interesting things which will deepen your understanding.

Casualty

He would drink by himself
And raise a weathered thumb
Towards the high shelf,
Calling another rum
And blackcurrant, without
Having to raise his voice,
Or order a quick stout
By a lifting of the eyes
And a discreet dumb-show
Of pulling off the top;
At closing time would go
In waders and peaked cap
Into the showery dark,
A dole-kept breadwinner
But a natural for work.
I loved his whole manner,
Sure-footed but not too sly,
His deadpan sidling tact,
His fisherman's quick eye
And turned observant back.

Incomprehensible
To him, my other life.
Sometimes, on his high stool,
Too busy with his knife
At a tobacco plug
And not meeting my eye,
In the pause after a slug
He mentioned poetry.
We would be on our own
And, always politic
And shy of condescension,
I would manage by some trick

To switch the talk to eels
Or lore of the horse and cart
Or the Provisionals.

But my tentative art
His turned back watches too:
He was blown to bits
Out drinking in a curfew
Others obeyed, three nights
After they shot dead
The thirteen men in Derry.
PARAS THIRTEEN, the walls said,
BOGSIDE NIL. That Wednesday
Everybody held
His breath and trembled.

II

It was a day of cold
Raw silence, wind-blown
Surplice and soutane:
Rained-on, flower-laden
Coffin after coffin
Seemed to float from the door
Of the packed cathedral
Like blossoms on slow water.
The common funeral
Unrolled its swaddling band,
Lapping, tightening
Till we were braced and bound
Like brothers in a ring.

But he would not be held
At home by his own crowd
Whatever threats were phoned,
Whatever black flags waved.
I see him as he turned
In that bombed offending place,
Remorse fused with terror
In his still knowable face,

His cornered outfaced stare
Blinding in the flash.

He had gone miles away
For he drank like a fish
Nightly, naturally
Swimming towards the lure
Of warm lit-up places,
The blurred mesh and murmur
Drifting among glasses
In the gregarious smoke.
How culpable was he
That last night when he broke
Our tribe's complicity?
'Now you're supposed to be
An educated man,'
I hear him say. 'Puzzle me
The right answer to that one.'

III

I missed his funeral,
Those quiet walkers
And sideways talkers
Shoaling out of his lane
To the respectable
Purring of the hearse . . .
They moved in equal pace
With the habitual
Slow consolation
Of a dawdling engine,
The line lifted, hand
Over fist, cold sunshine
On the water, the land
Banked under fog: that morning
I was taken in his boat,
The screw purling, turning
Indolent fathoms white,
I tasted freedom with him.
To get out early, haul

Steadily off the bottom,
Dispraise the catch, and smile
As you find a rhythm
Working you, slow mile by mile,
Into your proper haunt
Somewhere, well out, beyond . . .

Dawn-sniffing revenant,
Plodder through midnight rain,
Question me again.

If you are hooked on Heaney, as I hope you are by
now, you will find yourself comparing early poems such
as 'Digging', 'Follower' and 'Docker' with later ones such
as 'Casualty', 'Strange Fruit' and the 'Glanmore Sonnets'
and noting similarities *and* differences. You may even
have resolved to find out more about the man and his
work.

Glossary of literary terms used in this book

abstraction   general idea, or concept. Abstract words, such as truth or freedom, have a wider range of meaning than more concrete ones, such as daffodil or mouse. The reader or listener, however, faced with many possible 'meanings', is likely to have difficulty in forming a precise or 'sensible' image of the 'thing' to which the abstraction refers. Abstract language is directed to the mind rather than to the senses.

aesthetic   concerned with sensuous perception, particularly perception of what is beautiful.

alliteration   the repetition of a sound (usually one letter and nearly always a consonant). The alliterated sound often comes at the beginning of words. Various effects are to be achieved by alliteration: the letter *b* (common in abusive language) can be used to express force and frustration; *f* can suggest a disgusted or dismissive tone; *d*s and *t*s harden, firm up, a line; *l* gives liquidity to a line. Yeats's well-known 'I hear lake water lapping with low sounds by the shore' is an example of alliteration exploited to the limit, beyond which it would become ridiculous.

allusion   an indirect reference.

ambiguous   having more than one possible meaning (strictly two possible meanings – in Latin *ambi* means both). Ambiguities are often unintentional, errors in expression, but sometimes they are used deliberately for effect, particularly in poetry and other forms of literature.

ambivalence   the existence at one time in the one person of opposing emotional attitudes to the same object.

anthology   (from the Greek for 'a gathering of flowers') a collection of poems or prose extracts by different authors.

antithesis   obvious contrast.

apostrophise   to address an absent person, or personification, as if he or she were present.

archaism   an expression or style which has become out of date.

archetype   a perfect or typical example.

assonance the rhyming of the vowel sounds in one word with the vowel sounds in another.

ballad at one time, a song to accompany a dance. Now, the word applies to almost any simple song or poem which has a chorus or refrain. It also applies, more particularly, to narrative poems, especially those set in the iambic four line stanzas which are to be found in the Border Ballads.

bard a writer of lyric or heroic verse of a public nature. Formerly, in Celtic culture, a poet who wrote in praise of his clan and its chiefs.

biography an account of a person's life written by another. When the account is written by the person himself or herself it is an autobiography.

caesura a pause either for rhythm (in classical prosody) or for meaning (in modern poetry) which usually occurs near the middle of a line.

colloquial informal and conversational as opposed to formal and literary.

concrete the opposite of abstract (see abstraction). For comment on what is called 'concrete poetry' see the essay on Edwin Morgan's poetry.

connotation the denotation of a word is its principle, bare, meaning: its connotation is made up of the meanings normally associated with it. Thus, the word 'mother' denotes one who has given birth to a child while it connotes such ideas as affection, home, understanding, upbringing.

consonants the letters representing sounds which are in some way obstructed in the mouth or throat. All letters are consonants with the exception of the vowels *a e i o u*. The letters *w* and *y* are sometimes referred to as semi-vowels.

couplet two successive lines of verse which are of equal length and which rhyme with each other. In the heroic couplet the lines are comprised of iambic pentameter. (See prosody.)

critique review or criticism.

dialect the language spoken in a particular area, often by members of a particular social or occupational class.

dialogue a conversation between two (or more) people.

diction the choice and use of words.

didactic instructional. Often the instruction offered is of a moral nature. When the word is used in connection with literature, the implication usually is that the instruction is dull and out of place in a work of art which should be primarily a matter of imagined experience and feeling, not a lesson.

dissonance a combination of sounds in which the various contributory sounds do not blend harmoniously together.

eclectic selecting at will from different sources in what seems to be rather an arbitrary or haphazard way.

elegy a sad poem or song, usually a lament for the dead.

epigram originally, writing on a building or a tomb, but now the word is used to mean a short, witty piece of writing.

epigraph as for epigram, but in the form of a quotation at, for example, the beginning of a book.

epitaph an inscription on a tomb or monument or a speech or piece of writing composed to commemorate one who has died.

free verse verse which has no regular rhyme or metre.

gnomic full of short, truthful or apt, statements of a general nature. The word has by now been almost altogether replaced by the word aphoristic (noun, aphorism).

hedonism the pursuit of pleasure.

hyperbole exaggeration used for effect, not for the purpose of deceiving.

iambic See prosody.

image a picture in the mind's eye (or it could be a taste, touch or scent, or sound also 'pictured' in the mind) which conveys an idea to the reader or listener. One can usually get quickly into the setting and atmosphere of a poem by focusing attention on the images within it.

intonation   variation in the pitch (that is the height and depth of the note) of the voice. Statements are usually expressed in a falling pitch, questions in a rising one.

irony   the use of words to imply something contrary to what they normally mean.

juvenilia   works produced before the artist has attained a mature style.

literal   a word used literally is used to mean just what it plainly means – a rose is, literally, a flower on a bush. The word rose, on the other hand, when used to describe, to compliment, a lady is used figuratively. The lady may resemble a rose in some respects – colourful, tender, beautiful, fragrant – but she is not literally, in plain fact, a rose.

lyric   a short, frequently songlike, poem in which the writer expresses his own thoughts and feelings. (In classical Greece a lyric was a poem intended to be sung to the accompaniment of the lyre.) Nowadays, the word also applies to songs within a stage play or musical or to the words, as distinct from the music, of a song. The meaning of the word has become somewhat vague and 'vulgarised'.

metaphor   in a metaphor one thing, or action, is said to be another which in fact it only resembles in some respect, or respects. A metaphor may be fresh and sharp (And walked abroad in a shower of all my days) or it may be dull and overworked (a tower of strength); it may be short or it may be extended as in the case of MacCaig's poem 'Smuggler'; it may be fully expressed (She was a right old hen with them) or it may be only implied (She cackled around the rooms incessantly). There are many other things metaphors may or may not be – mixed, misleading, inept (She was a swan on the dance floor – webbed feet?). Metaphor is widespread throughout nearly all forms of language – poetry, newspaper reporting, scientific discourse, daily conversation – and, well used, it contributes greatly to the vitality and growth of language. It is forever bringing similarities to notice and determining the ways in which we think of aspects of the world around us. (See also simile.)

metaphysical   metaphysics is a branch of philosophy in which attempts are made to understand the ultimate nature of things knowable to man. Metaphysical is a word very loosely used in ordinary, as distinct from philosophical, discourse to refer to all sorts of theorising and speculation of a deep or ambitious, or obscure, nature.

metre   see prosody.

monosyllabic having one syllable.

myth a story or belief which, though purporting to be true, has no truth in it, at least no literal truth.

octave a unit of eight lines in poetry, usually the first eight lines in a sonnet.

onomatopoeia the reflection in the sound of a word of the sound of the occurrence to which the word refers. e.g. tinkle, screech, flapping.

parable a short story which makes use of familiar events to convey a moral or a religious message.

parody an exaggerated imitation intended to make fun of the original.

personification in personification things which are not human (creatures, flowers, stars, machines . . .) or abstract ideas (Freedom, Faith, Justice . . .) are spoken of or written of as if they felt and behaved like people.

philistine uncultured and materialistic.

prosody the study of the art of versification, of metre and of rhyme. This is a large subject. Here only a limited amount of comment upon some of the most obvious features of rhyme and metre is possible.
RHYME Popularly defined (the traditional definition is precise and rather restrictive) rhyme is the sameness of sound in the last syllables of words, when they are placed close enough to each other on the page for this sameness to be noticeable. Various forms of rhyme are to be encountered, among which are: full rhyme (wings/things; falling/calling); half-rhyme (or para, i.e. near rhyme) (groined/groaned; bestirred/stared); end rhyme (at the end of lines); internal rhyme (in the course of lines, often near the middle). In Owen's 'Strange Meeting' we have an example of both half rhyme and internal rhyme in the line 'And by his smile, I knew that sullen hall'. For an illustration of one particular rhyme scheme, see the entry on the sonnet.
METRE Rhythm in poetry is created by the arrangement of words into stressed and unstressed, long or short, syllables. Metre is the term used to denote particular, regular, arrangements. The unstressed or short syllable in a metre or a rhythm is marked in scansion (i.e. the analysis of the metre) by a breve (˘) and the stressed or long syllable by a macron (-). The groupings of stressed and unstressed syllables are called feet (rather like bars in music). The

most common foot in English poetry is the iambic one which consists of an unstressed syllable followed by a stressed one,
The kind of feet and the number of feet in a line determine the kind of metre in the poem. Thus,

Whŏse woŏds/thĕse āre/Ĭ thĭnk/Ĭ knōw (Frost) is iambic tetrameter (4 feet)
while

Ĭf Ĭ/wĕre fiērce,/ănd bāld,/ănd shōrt/ŏf breāth, (Sassoon) is iambic pentameter (5 feet)
One foot is called monometer, two dimeter and three trimeter. (Notice that the spelling of metre on its own is different from when the word is incorporated into longer ones.)
Other common metres are the trochaic (ˉ ˘) which is a free running, 'tripping' sort of metre often to be found in light verse and the dactyllic (ˉ ˘ ˘). The opening lines of Hardy's poem 'The Voice' flow beautifully in dactylls. One might consider, too, how much smoother and more natural 'Dulce et decorum est pro patria mori' would sound if it were recognised to be basically dactyllic and not iambic!

pun the use of words and phrases to gain effect from their ambiguities. Punning, though commonly derided, may be lively and creative.

quatrain a stanza, or poem, consisting of four lines which, in many cases, rhyme alternately.

refrain a regularly recurring phrase or line. A refrain which consists of several lines is called a chorus.

renaissance rebirth, revival.

requiem a piece of music composed as a memorial to a dead person.

rhetoric usually, the act of using speech to influence people. Rhetorical speech is often under suspicion of being over-ornamental, contrived, empty of real meaning.

rhyme see prosody.

rhythm see prosody.

run-on lines the flowing on of a sentence from one line into the next in poetry. Sometimes this is referred to as enjambment. The opposite of end-stopped lines.

satire   the use of ridicule and/or irony to draw attention to the folly or wickedness thought to be present in some person, institution or idea.

sestet   a unit of six lines of poetry, usually the last six lines in a sonnet.

simile   simile is akin to metaphor, but it is less concise and less frequently used. In it the comparison made is signalled by the word 'as' or the word 'like'. 'High on the hillside the church stood like a rock.'

sonnet   a poem of fourteen lines, each line containing five iambic feet. There are two main types of sonnet (*i*) the Petrarchan in which the rhyme scheme is abbaabba/cdecde. The break between the octave and the sestet here is called the *volta*. (*ii*) the Shakesperean in which the rhyme scheme is abab cdcd efef gg, i.e. four quatrains and a couplet. The sonnet has been an exceptionally popular and long-lasting form in poetry.

stanza   two or more lines in poetry forming a unit, rather like a paragraph in prose. Traditionally, stanzas within a poem are of the same pattern in terms of metre and rhyme. The word verse, although originally it meant one line, is now used to refer to units in a poem which may, or may not, be of the same pattern.

style   a very general term meaning the way in which something is done, the way, therefore, in which a poem is written.

syllable   a part of a word that can be pronounced by itself. The word 'moon' has one syllable (is monosyllabic) while the word 'sunlit' has two (disyllabic).

symbol   a thing which stands for or represents something other than itself. A symbol may be a matter of choice and design (e.g. the symbol for British Rail) or it may be chosen because it is in fact associated with that which it symbolises (e.g. a daffodil for Spring).

syntax   the order or arrangement of words in a sentence or, more generally, in a language.

theme   the idea or topic at the centre of a discourse, discussion, poem, etc.

tone   this is a word which has many different meanings in different contexts – music, speech, physiology, art . . . . In a literary context it refers to the manner in which the writer addresses the reader – bitter, ironic, witty, didactic, confidential and so on.

universal   relating to the whole of a class of things. In a literary context it usually means relating to the whole of mankind ('He writes only of people in Forfar, but the message which comes across has universal significance.') Claims to universality in literature are best to be treated with caution: people are very various and there are many corners in the world.

vowels   see consonants.

Acknowledgements

The contributors, editor and publishers are grateful to the following for permission to reproduce the extracts indicated:
Boosey & Hawkes Music Publishers Ltd for the extract from Benjamin Britten's *War Requiem*; Canongate Publishing Ltd for 'A Highland Woman' by Sorley Maclean; Jonathan Cape Ltd for the extracts from *The Poetry of Robert Frost* edited by Edward Connery Latham; Carcanet Press Ltd for the extracts from *Poems of Thirty Years* © Edwin Morgan 1982; Chatto & Windus for the extracts from *Autobiography* by Edwin Muir; Iain Crichton Smith for the extracts from his poems formerly published by Eyre and Spottiswoode in *Thistles and Roses* (1961 & 1977) and *New Poets* (1959), and to MacDonald Publishers for his poems from *The Long River* (1955), *Lines Review* No 21, *The Law and the Grace* (1965), and *The Permanent Island* (1975); Faber & Faber Ltd for the extracts from *Field Work* by Seamus Heaney, *Lupercal* by Ted Hughes, and *The Collected Poems of Edwin Muir*; Hogarth Press for the extracts from *Selected Poems* and *Fishermen with Ploughs* by George Mackay Brown, and *A Common Grace, A Man in My Position, Riding Lights, Rings on a Tree, Surroundings* and *A World of Difference* by Norman MacCaig; MacDonald Publishers for the extracts from the poems of Derick Thomson; John Murray (Publishers) Ltd for the extracts from *Collected Poems* by John Betjeman.

Permission to reproduce photographs on the pages listed below is also gratefully acknowledged:
Jonathan Cape Ltd 49; Mansell Collection 7; Jessie Ann Matthew 120; National Portrait Gallery 18, 34, 37, 75, 87; Universal Pictorial Press 66, 95, 189.
Other photographs © Oliver & Boyd (photographer Angus Blackburn).

While every effort has been made to trace copyright owners, the publishers apologise for any omissions in the above list.